WHSmith

Revision

English

**Ray Barker and
Roger Machin**

**Age 11–14
Years 7–9**
Key Stage 3

Hachette UK's policy is to use papers that are natural, renewable and recyclable products and made from wood grown in sustainable forests. The logging and manufacturing processes are expected to conform to the environmental regulations of the country of origin.

Orders: please contact Bookpoint Ltd, 130 Milton Park, Abingdon, Oxon OX14 4SB. Telephone: (44) 01235 827720. Fax: (44) 01235 400454. Lines are open 9.00a.m.–5.00p.m., Monday to Saturday, with a 24-hour message answering service. Visit our website at www.hoddereducation.co.uk.

© Ray Barker and Roger Machin 2013
First published in 2007 exclusively for WHSmith by
Hodder Education
An Hachette UK Company
338 Euston Road
London NW1 3BH

This second edition first published in 2013 exclusively for WHSmith by Hodder Education.

Impression number   10 9 8 7 6 5 4
Year   2018 2017 2016 2015 2014

This edition has been updated, 2014, to reflect National Curriculum changes.

Cover illustration by Oxford Designers and Illustrators Ltd
All other illustrations by Fakenham Prepress Solutions, Fakenham, Norfolk NR21 8NN
Typeset in 10pt Helvetica Neue by Fakenham Prepress Solutions, Fakenham, Norfolk NR21 8NN
Printed in Spain

A catalogue record for this title is available from the British Library.

ISBN: 978 1444 189 315

Contents

Section C: Dealing with literature

How to use this book

The fact that you are choosing to read these words means you are thinking about improving your English. Congratulations! This is the first step towards success and you have taken it already. Your desire to succeed is the essential ingredient to progress. Think of this book as your partner, your personal trainer, in your quest to achieve.

Key Stage 3

Key Stage 3 (you'll often see it called just KS3) is the name given to Years 7, 8 and 9. Students in KS3 are normally aged between 11 and 14 years old. It is a crucial time for all subjects and no less so for English. It is the time when the lessons learned from junior school are built upon and when the foundations are laid for study up to GCSE. Almost all students do the compulsory KS3 tests at the end of Year 9. Many schools now opt to take similar tests at the end of Years 7 and 8.

English at KS3

The English tests at KS3 assess students in two basic areas: their ability to read and write. Teachers assess the other two components of English (speaking and listening) separately. Students are expected to read lots of different sorts of texts (for example, stories, newspapers, biographies) and to show their understanding of them. They are expected to demonstrate that they can write in a variety of ways (for example, imaginatively, persuasively, informatively) and in good English.

Revision

Many students think of revision as something they do just before a test takes place. Don't be one of them! Success is based on continual revision, just a little every day. Go over what you know. Check, recheck and identify areas of difficulty. Practise what you're good at and get help in areas where you're weaker. Let this book be your friend and companion in this process. An exercise every day or two – more if you're enjoying yourself – will be enough to build up your confidence and ability. Successful revision is like effective physical training: it needs to be gradual.

Using this book

Work through the units in the order they appear. In other words, start with Unit 1 and finish with Unit 85. The reason for this is that the skills learned and revised earlier in the book are built upon as the text progresses. There is no fixed time limit for each unit although you should be able to finish most of them in a single sitting. Towards the end of each of the units you will find a more challenging section (shaded in mauve). This section is designed to help you push yourself that little bit further in the direction of understanding and success. The Revision booster boxes and Revision tips at the side also help with your study.

Home study tips

You'll discover fairly quickly that the answers are at the end of the book! Try not to look at them until you have worked as hard as you possibly can on the unit. The fact that you are working at home means you are eager to improve and to get ahead. You're not going to do this if you take the easy way out. Engage with what you read, and write answers as fully and in as much detail as you can. Remember that you are taking responsibility for your own learning. Not many students do this and if you do it properly it is going to give you an advantage.

If you work steadily through this book your English will improve. This is a definite, cast-iron and unarguable fact. It might seem hard at first, especially if you're tired after a long day's work. But stick with it. Mental stamina, just like physical stamina, improves with exercise. Don't get downhearted if you can't complete an exercise. Give it your best shot and if you're still stuck in a rut, move on to another unit. Remember that the best way to get ahead is to get started and you're about to get started right now!

1: All sorts of nouns

In this unit you will learn
▶ to understand the varieties of nouns

Get started

Nouns are words that refer to people, places, things, ideas and feelings.

Common nouns are nouns that we can sense as part of our world. They are the sorts of nouns people talk about when they say that *a noun is a person, a place or a thing*.

Here is a list of common nouns.

water   fire   egg   atom   brick   hair   sugar   dragon   mouse   church

Notice that a thing doesn't actually have to be real to qualify as a common noun. Nor do you have to be able to sense it yourself.

Practice

1 a Which noun in the above list of common nouns exists only in stories?
       dragon
     b Which noun from the list above can only be sensed with special equipment?
       atom

2 a Pick out five common nouns from the list below.

apple   thinking   although   star   because   bag
colourful   sand   finger   unhappily

     b Read the following extract and write down the ten common nouns it contains.

> The farmer put down his hand and felt for the keys. Under the floor, in a hole in the earth, was a yellowing map. A mouse peeped out, with twitching nose and curious eyes.

2b
farmer
keys
floor
earth
map
mouse
nose
eyes
hand
hole

Abstract nouns are nouns that no one can identify in a physical sort of way. They can't be touched or seen. They are the sorts of words people mean when they talk about nouns referring to *thoughts, feelings and ideas*.

Here is a list of abstract nouns.

emptiness   sorrow   idea   passion   emotion   hate
energy   compliment   quantity   condition

Abstract nouns may look very different from common nouns. When you use them in sentences, though, it is much easier to spot their similarities. Look at the following pairs.

Unless they are used to start a sentence, common and abstract nouns begin with a small letter.

The well was deep.   *His sorrow was deep.*

The apple is sweet.   *Revenge is sweet.*

It was a wonderful day.   *It was a wonderful idea.*

3 Write down the three common nouns and the three abstract nouns used in the examples above. well and deep
apple and sweet
day and wonderful

Proper nouns are special types of nouns that always begin with a capital letter. They are nouns that identify *particular* people, places, countries, continents, days, months, schools, businesses and so on. Here is a list of proper nouns.

Asia Annie Eid Monday Cyprus Mr Tumnus
February Microsoft Glasgow Everest

Nouns used as titles (of books, plays, films) are classed as proper nouns and need capital letters.

The Incredibles   The Lord of the Rings   Jurassic Park

Collective nouns are nouns that describe collections of things.

a **pack** of wolves   a **pair** of shoes

a **bunch** of grapes   a **troop** of monkeys

a **collection** of comics   a **flock** of seagulls

Collective nouns allow us to think of lots of individual things as one single group.

Read the following sentences.

Jo read the book.

The orange is in the bowl.

The excitement flowed over at the end of the game.

The plans were given to the team of engineers.

On Saturday the girls are going to Moscow.

His disappointment was clear to the crowd of onlookers.

4 a Find at least five common nouns.
   book, orange, bowl, crowd, engineers
   b Identify two abstract nouns.
   ~~Moscow~~, excitement, dissapointment
   c Find three proper nouns.
   Moscow, Saturday, Jo
   d Find two collective nouns.
   team, crowd

How did I do?

I understand the varieties of nouns.

7

2: Verbs in sentences

In this unit you will learn
▶ to explore the structure of sentences

Get started

Verbs are words that refer to actions, feelings and states. The following is a list of verbs.

grow shout slide flow play touch cry run slam arrive

Verbs provide information about what is done in a sentence.

Verbs are basic to sentences. Almost all sentences contain at least one verb in combination with a noun. The following noun + verb combinations use the first six verbs from the list above.

Plants **grow**.   Rivers **flow**.

Jonas **shouts**.   The kitten **plays**.

The children **slide**.   Hands **touch**.

Notice that the letter *s* has been added to the end of verbs where the noun before it (the subject) is in the third person. If you can replace a noun with the words *he*, *she* or *it*, then it is in the third person singular. Try this with the two examples above where an *s* has been added to the verb.

Practice

1 Make noun + verb combinations using the final four verbs from the list above. Try to use the third person in at least two of your sentences.

The babies cry, the kids run, the door slams
the guests arrive

Determiners are small words placed before nouns. They help determine how the noun is understood. The following sentences are identical except for their determiners.

A kitten plays.   The kitten plays.   My kitten plays.

Changing the determiner alters the way a reader understands *kitten*.

Other determiners are

some your this that his their those its these

2 Add appropriate determiners to make new sentences from each of the following.

plants grow   rivers flow   hands touch

Some plants   The rivers   Their hands
grow   flow   touch

Identifying verbs is sometimes a problem when students think they need to look for a single word. It is true that verbs can often be made up of just one word, but they can be made up of as many as four.

*The clown **laughed**.*

is an example of the basic sentence structure

determiner + noun + verb

So are the following.

*The clown **has laughed**.*	(two-word verb)
*The clown **has been laughing**.*	(three-word verb)
*The clown **will have been laughing**.*	(four-word verb)

All the words after *The clown* are to do with the action of laughing, so they are included as part of the verb.

3 In each of the following sentences identify

   a the determiner (if there is one)

   [handwritten: 1.) Some   2.) A   3.) X   4.) The   5.) Most]

   b the noun

   [handwritten: 1.) people   2.) mole   3.) Gary   4.) audience   5.) monkeys]

   c the verb

   [handwritten: 1.) driving   2.) digging   3.) sings   4.) listening   5.) climb]

   Some people are driving.

   A mole has been digging.

   Gary sings.

   The audience will have been listening.

   Most monkeys climb.

Revision booster

The basic sentence structure described in this unit is

determiner + noun + verb

4 Add appropriate words to each of the following sentences so that this basic structure is completed. Don't forget that your verbs can be longer than a single word in length.

Some (lious) roar.

(My) birds (tweet).

(The) snow has been falling.

How did I do?

I can explore the structure of sentences.

3: Verb forms

In this unit you will learn
 ▶ to work with different verb forms

Get started

Verbs are words that refer to actions or states.

*She **kicked** the ball.   They **auctioned** the statue.   Kurtis **seems** unhappy.*

The first two verbs refer to the *actions* of kicking and auctioning. The third verb refers to the *state* of seeming to be something.

Practice

1 Identify the (single-word) verbs in each of the following sentences.

Davinia locked the door.

Alberto brings home fish every day.

She appears not to care.

I often think about it.

They smashed into each other on the ice rink.

Verbs change their form according to certain fixed rules. The infinitive form is used after the preposition *to*.

to laugh   to cry   to fall   to grow   to seem

It makes no sense to say *to locked,* so you know that *locked* is not the infinitive form.

2 Put each of the five verbs from question 1 into the infinitive form.

to lock, to bring, to appear, to think, to smash

Verbs also change their form according to the tense they are in.

I try   is a present tense form

I tried   is a past tense form

I will try   is a future tense form

I begin
I began
I will begin

3 Put the following verbs into the present, past and future tenses. Use the pronoun *I* as in the examples.

go   bring   have   begin

I go   I bring   I have
I went   I brought   I had
I will go   I will bring   I will have

Although English has different tenses to indicate different times (past, present and future) these divisions are not at all rigid. It is possible to say, for example,

I fly to Paris tomorrow morning.

This is obviously the present tense (of the verb *fly*) to refer to something that is going to happen in the future. This is not uncommon. You have also probably read or heard something like this.

Their boy dives and the ref gives a penalty. We weren't going to win after that.

In this case, the verbs *dives* and *gives* are used in the present tense to refer to something that happened in the past.

Remember that the expressions *past*, *present* and *future* are general descriptions of the uses of verb tense. You need to look at the context (how and where the verb is being used) to understand exactly what time is being referred to in each case.

The word *will* is used before the infinitive form of a main verb to create the future tense. Other modal verbs alter or modify the meanings of main verbs in different ways. Modal verbs are typically placed before the verb they modify.

can will might should could must may would

4 Identify the modal verbs and the main verbs in each of the following sentences.

In a few days they will come to Dublin.
        will , come
A few words might help.
        might , help
I can see what's wrong.
        can , see
Sally could buy herself a ticket.
        could , buy
Martin would wait outside every night without fail.
        would wait

The verb *will* is an example of a **modal verb**. Modal verbs are followed by the infinitive form of a main verb.

Revision booster

Look again at the list of eight modal verbs above. Use each of them in turn before the main verb *enjoy* in the following sentence. Notice how the meaning of the sentence is modified slightly on each occasion.

I enjoy myself.

How did I do?

I can work with different verb forms.

4: Using tenses

In this unit you will learn

▶ to express past and present time

Get started

Verbs change their forms to express when actions take place.

The following verbs are in the simple present tense.

*smile/smiles begin/begins am/are/is have/has
take/takes do/does think/thinks*

There are two different forms of each verb except for the verb *be* which has three forms. These forms must *agree* with the subject used in the sentence. The form of the verb that takes the letter *s* at the end has a third person singular subject. The third person singular is represented by the pronouns *he, she* or *it*. So the verb needs to agree with the subject as in the following examples.

She smiles It begins The cake is He has John takes Melanie thinks

The forms of the verb without the letter *s* at the end are used with subjects that are not third person singular. These are represented by the pronouns *I, you, we* and *they*.

I smile You are We have They think

The only verb that has a special form for the first person *I* is the verb *be*.

I am

Practice

The simple present tense is often used in passages that describe familiar or repeated actions. For example

> *I have my breakfast while my brother uses the shower. We always leave the house together. The walk to school takes forty minutes. We often meet different friends on the way. I am usually quite happy during this part of the morning.*

Subjects and verbs are often learned together in the following order

1 *I am*

2 *you are*

3 *he/she/it is.*

This traditional order is the reason why people refer to these pairings in their turn as *first person, second person* and *third person.*

❶ a Write down each of the six present tense verbs used in this passage.
have, uses, leave, meet, ~~takes walk~~ I am

b Which two of the verbs are used in the third person singluar?
~~uses~~ ~~and~~
uses and takes

You have identified two verbs as being in the third person singular. This is because they have changed their form (added an *s*) to *agree* with third person singular subjects.

Look at the subject of these two verbs. One is a two-word noun phrase and one is a four-word noun phrase.

② Replace each of these noun phrases with its appropriate pronoun.

[handwritten: ~~She~~ he uses and ~~they~~ takes]

The simple past tense has fewer variations than the simple present. Here are some examples of simple past tense verb forms.

bought   smiled   ran   was/were   had   coughed   mended   slipped   swam

Each of the verbs has a single past tense form except for the verb *be*. The verb *be* is formed as *was* in the first and third person singular.

③ Change the verb forms to express the following sentences in the simple past tense.

a *I buy lemons at the market.*

[handwritten: I bought]

b *You are really funny.*

[handwritten: You were]

c *It looks ready to rain.*

[handwritten: It looked]

d *His mobile irritates me.*

[handwritten: His mobile irritated me.]

e *The tiny spider spins a delicate web.*

[handwritten: Spun]

> The simple past tense is used to express completed events. It is a common form in telling stories and relating experiences.
>
> Read the following account. It is written using simple past tense verbs.
>
> > The buzzard flew to the highest peak. It looked down on the valley below. This mighty bird was indeed a fearful beast. Suddenly, it swooped down into the crevice. It emerged a few moments later with some small mammal in its beak.

④ Write down the five simple past tense verbs used in the passage.

[handwritten: flew, looked, was, swooped, emerged]

Revision booster

⑤ Rewrite the buzzard passage changing all the verbs into the simple present tense.

⑥ Now read the passage through in its simple present form. Where might you hear a description of an animal's behaviour expressed in this way?

How did I do?

I can express past and present time.

[handwritten: ✓ checkbox ticked]

5: Infinitives

In this unit you will learn
▶ to understand infinitive forms

Get started

Recall the different forms of the verb you have already studied. You have seen how a verb like *throw* can alter its spelling and combine with other words to adapt to different functions.

throw

throws	(third person singular)
threw	(past tense)
am throwing/was throwing	(present continuous/past continuous)
have thrown/had thrown	(present perfect/past perfect)

Practice

1 Make a list just the same as the one above for the following verbs

a *speak* speaks, spoke, am speaking/was speaking have spoken/had spoken

b *fly* flies, flew, am flying/was flying, have flown/had flown

The **infinitive** form of the verb is not related to a subject. Look at the list above. All the different forms of the verb (but one) need to have a subject in order to make sense. The infinitive form *throw* doesn't refer to a subject. Its reference is therefore **infinite**.

In the case of almost all English verbs, the infinitive is the same as the first person form. So, *throw* (the infinitive) is in the same form as *throw* (the finite verb) used with the pronoun *I*. The exception to this rule is the verb *be*. *Be* (the infinitive) is in a different form to *am* (a finite form of the verb) used with the pronoun *I*.

2 Write down the infinitive form of each of these verbs. The first is done for you.

was approaching	approach
had felt	~~felt~~ feel
are	~~are~~ be
is creaking	creak
has grown	grow
smashes	smash

> **!** The infinitive is often expressed as a phrase that follows the preposition *to*. This communicates the idea of an abstract action (*to hide, to whisper, to be*) that is not connected with a *subject* or *doer*.

The infinitive is important because it is the *root* form of the verb. It is the form from which all the other forms are developed. You need to understand the infinitive in order to be able to develop verb tenses and spell correctly.

Read the following passage by a well-known cookery writer.

> Take the chicken and cover it in garlic butter. Turn the oven on and leave it for twenty minutes. Smash the salt grains with your mortar and pestle. Roll the chicken thoroughly in the salt. Place in the oven and wait for this delicious roast.

This is a form of writing that instructs. The cookery writer is providing the reader with the instructions that are needed to prepare and bake a chicken. The sentences are all in what is called the **imperative** form. That is, they use an infinitive to give directions and they do not refer directly to a subject. Here are some examples of imperative forms.

Stay calm after an accident.   *Put* it away in the box.

Taste the food immediately.   *Be* careful and **come** again soon.

There is an understood 'modal verb' before each infinitive, e.g. *You should* be careful.

Notice that the last sentence contains two imperative verbs. When two verbs are used like this they are said to form two **imperative clauses**. In the cookery instructions, there are three sentences that contain two imperative clauses.

3 In all, the passage has eight verbs, all used in the imperative form. Write down each one of them.

take, cover, turn, leave
smash, roll, place, wait

Imperatives are used for instructions because they are straight and to the point. For the same reason, they can be used to signal a kind of friendly directness. For example,

Would you like to come over?   can be framed as the imperative
Come over!

4 Turn the following questions into imperatives.

Will you have something to eat?
have something to eat
Would you like to take a seat?
take a seat
Why don't you come in and enjoy yourself?
come in and enjoy yourself

How did I do?

I understand infinitive forms.

6: Active and passive

In this unit you will learn
▶ to distinguish between text types

Get started

The earthquake struck at exactly 11.32. Measuring 7.2 on the Richter Scale this was the most devastating of all the earthquakes to hit California in modern history. The scale of the destruction was immense. 2000 homes were destroyed, 370 miles of road were made impassable and eight bridges were so seriously damaged they had to be pulled down.

Practice

1 a Where did this earthquake strike?

California

b What did it measure on the Richter Scale?

7-2

c How many miles of road did the earthquake make impassable?

370 miles

This is an informative text. It provides lots of detailed information in relatively few lines.

2 a How does the first sentence add to the impression of precision?

It's being an exactly and not rounded

b Where would you expect to find this sort of informative text?

Geography case study

Look at the following phrases.

2000 homes were destroyed

eight bridges were damaged

They are **passive** because the thing or person that does the acting is not mentioned.

Look at these two passive phrases from different informative texts.

Yellow is mixed with blue to make green

Grapes are grown on south-facing slopes

The important information is about the process. The reader doesn't need to know that

The painter mixes yellow and blue to make green

The farmer grows grapes on south-facing slopes

In the informative text above, the reader does not need to be reminded that the earthquake caused the destruction. What is interesting is the destruction it caused.

> ⓘ Writers organise sentences in different ways to suit each different text.

3 Make these active sentences passive.

a *The earthquake destroyed three dams. Three dams were ...* destroyed

b *It devastated 2400 square miles.* 2400 square miles ... were devastated

c *It caused $430 million of damage.* $430 million caused by damage

---

Read this account of the same earthquake.

> I first became aware of a sort of rattling sound just after I'd gone to bed. I was half asleep and had some idea that my partner was downstairs washing up. Then there was this terrible bang that sounded like a bomb or a rocket or some kind of unearthly explosion.
>
> 'My God,' I thought. 'We're being invaded.'
>
> I pulled on a shirt and ran downstairs. Nothing could have prepared me for the scene of utter devastation that lay outside. My car was upside down in the drive, the telegraph wires were down, there was a crater where my neighbour's house had been. And all around us still, there was this terrible shuddering and an eerie orange glow ...

This passage sets out to describe the earthquake. It provides lots of personal detail and gives the reader a sense of what being caught up in the earthquake was like.

4 a What does the writer think at the very start of the earthquake?

It is his partner washing up

b What does he think when he is woken properly by the explosion?

that they were being invaded

The writer uses lots of adjective/noun combinations to describe just how he felt as the earthquake struck. The first of these is *rattling sound* at the beginning of the description.

5 Write down two more adjective/noun combinations that describe what the writer heard. terrible bang / eerie orange / unearthly explosion

---

Revision booster

In the final paragraph of the second extract, the writer describes three things that have been damaged by the earthquake.

6 a What are the three things the writer describes?

b Why would these things not be described in the first extract?

7 What is the point of having two such different pieces of writing to describe exactly the same thing?

How did I do?

I know how to distinguish between text types.

7: Using pronouns

In this unit you will learn
- ▶ to identify pronouns and their functions

Get started

Look at this sentence.

Kiera was shopping when Kiera fainted.

The proper noun, Kiera, is repeated and it sounds odd. To avoid this sort of repetition, writers use **pronouns**. Pronouns are words that substitute for nouns. Pronouns stand in place of nouns so that nouns do not get repeated over and over again.

*Kiera was shopping when **she** fainted.*

This is a much better sentence that seems far more natural.

The most common pronouns are **personal pronouns**. The personal pronouns are

I/me   you   he/him   she/her   it   we/us   they/them

They are used to help us avoid strings of sentences like this.

Amri opened the door. The door creaked noisily. Amri walked into the kitchen and looked at the golden egg cups. Shakily, Amri reached out for the golden egg cups. The writer of these words dashed into the room before Amri could go any further.

Using pronouns improves the effect.

*Amri opened the door. **It** creaked noisily. **He** walked into the kitchen and looked at the golden egg cups. Shakily, **he** reached out for **them**. **I** dashed into the room before **he** could go any further.*

Practice

1 Rewrite this short passage using personal pronouns to improve the effect.

Gemma looked at the stars. The stars shone brightly down on Gemma, bathing Gemma in silvery light. Gemma stirred as Gemma felt the wind. The wind rustled through the trees. Shadows formed in the twilight. Shadows seemed somehow kind and gentle.

You must also be able to identify **possessive pronouns**. Possessive pronouns indicate ownership or possession. They are

mine   yours   his   hers   its   ours   theirs

Possessive pronouns indicate possession but they do not take apostrophes.

They help writers avoid sentences like

*That frisbee has been **my frisbee** for ages but **your frisbee** is just as good.*

2 Rewrite the sentence above using possessive pronouns to improve the style.

That frisbee has been mine for ages but yours is just as good

The third type of pronoun covered in this unit is **reflexive pronouns**. The reflexive pronouns are

myself   yourself/yourselves   himself/herself/itself   ourselves   themselves

They are used like this.

We are not too unhappy with ourselves.

After four hours I gave myself a break.

3 Rewrite the following sentences using reflexive pronouns.

The athletes ran the athletes into the ground.

The athletes ran themselves into the ground

I am unhappy with the writer of this sentence.

I am unhappy with myself.

The washing up won't do the washing up.

The washing up won't do itself

Pronouns refer back to nouns. Readers must be able to identify the **reference** of a pronoun. In the following sentence, for example, the pronoun reference is unclear.

The ant and the bee fought outside the nest. It won within moments.

Who won the fight? The reader is not told because the writer assumes too much. The reference of the pronoun *it* is unclear. This is a very common error which you must avoid.

4 In the following passage, identify the

a personal pronouns

he, I, him, she, they.

b possessive pronouns

mine

c reflexive pronouns

themselves

> The gargoyle looked down from the side of the house. Although he was mine, I thought him extremely ugly. Stephanie loved all gargoyles. She liked the idea that people once believed they could protect themselves by carving monsters on walls.

How did I do?

I know how to identify pronouns and their functions.

19

8: Pronouns in action

Get started

This is an extract from the start of a letter that campaigns against the siting of a nuclear waste dump near to local housing.

> You may have heard that the government is planning a nuclear waste dump in the countryside just out of town. Skipham Residents' Association consider this to be completely unacceptable. We believe strongly that all of us must all stand together to oppose this threat.

Pronouns are words that make reference to nouns.

Instead of *The girl is friendly* we can write *She is friendly*.

Instead of *Anna and Hero are walking* we can write *They are walking*.

Pronouns include the words

I   you   he   she   it   we   they   me   him   her   us   them

Practice

The names Robbie, Mollie and Arun are proper nouns. So is Skipham Residents' Association. They are special names for people, towns, days of the week, businesses and so on. They always start with a capital letter. The pronouns that replace these proper nouns *do not* start with a capital letter, with the single exception of the pronoun *I*.

1 Replace the highlighted nouns with pronouns.

a Give the bread to **Robbie**. *him*

b **Mollie** is running towards **Arun and Stevie**. *She* *them*

c **Mollie** gave **the phone** to **Carla**. *She* *it* *her*

2 Rewrite this extract from the letter above, replacing the highlighted nouns with the appropriate pronoun.

the government is planning **a nuclear waste dump in the countryside** just out of **town**

The extract you have just been asked to write should be impossible to understand. This is because readers need to know what noun a pronoun has replaced. They need to know what a pronoun is referring to.

Read this sentence.

Pollution is bad: it must be stopped.

It is clear to the reader that the pronoun *it* refers to the word *pollution.*

3 a Write down the three pronouns contained in the nuclear waste passage. *we us you*

b What does each of these pronouns refer to?

The following extract from the letter gives the reader lots of information about the *dump* in a very few words.

a nuclear waste dump in the countryside just out of town

The information is built up like this:

● The main noun is *dump.*

● The descriptive adjectives *nuclear* and *waste* tell us what kind of dump it is.

● The phrase *in the countryside* tells us where the dump is.

● The next phrase *just out of town* tells us in more detail where the dump is.

The following phrases develop nouns in the same way.

the red ladder in the cupboard under the stairs

the broken roundabout at the park near the sea

the overripe banana in the bowl on the table

4 a Write down the main noun (a single word) in each of these three phrases.

b What are the three adjectives used to add detail to each of the nouns?

Revision booster

5 Add detail to the following phrases using the structures given.

a the (adjective) painting in the (second noun) near the (third noun)

b the (adjective) sunshine on the (second noun) at the (third noun)

How did I do?

I know how to work with nouns and pronouns.

9: Prepositions in phrases

In this unit you will learn
▸ to expand phrases with prepositions

Get started

Prepositions are words that go before nouns and pronouns. They tell us about the relationships between things.

Here is a list of some words often used as prepositions.

in under on beneath beside with over through round inside at around

Changing prepositions changes the way things relate to each other. Look at the following example.

*The ball flew **into** the goal.*

*The ball flew **over** the goal.*

The relationship between the ball and the goal (and the meaning of the sentence) is altered in an important way just by changing the preposition.

Practice

1 Change the preposition (only the preposition) to alter the meanings of the following sentences.

*The dog was **under** the table.*

*Thomas played **on** the sand.*

*She arrived well **before** the start of the concert.*

Writers can build up relationships between nouns by using prepositions carefully.

*The dog **with** one eye was **under** the table **in** the hall.*

The preposition *with* tells us about the relationship between the dog and its eye.

The preposition *in* relates the table to the hall.

The dog with one eye is a **noun phrase**. It does not contain a verb and it can be replaced in the sentence with a pronoun. Reread the sentence but replace the noun phrase with the pronoun *he*, *she* or *it*. In most cases, you can identify a noun phrase by replacing it with a pronoun and checking that the sentence still makes sense.

The second noun phrase in the sentence is *the table in the hall*. Replace it with a pronoun to check that the sentence still makes sense.

The following sentence contains two noun phrases and two prepositions.

The skull with its sinister grin watched the boat on the water.

The two noun phrases are *The skull with its sinister grin* and *the boat on the water*.

The two prepositions are *with* and *on*.

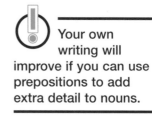

2   a   What is *the skull* related to by the preposition *with*?

     b   Which two nouns are related by the preposition *on*?

3   In each of the following sentences identify the

     a   noun phrases

     b   prepositions

The girl in the red coat ran through the gates of the city.

There may be worm holes in space.

'Men in Black' is a film with a message.

A rat without a tail slipped between the legs of the chair.

4   Look at the nouns (or determiners + nouns) in the left-hand column. Match them with the phrases in the right-hand column to make ten complete noun phrases.

The fish	*above the Earth*
The ship	*without a proper blade*
A knife	*in the pond*
The secret cupboard	*on the dirty pavement*
Alice	*beneath your feet*
The broken glass	*behind the wall*
Clouds	*with the sail*
Caves	*on the seat beside you*
The ground	*in Wonderland*
The cat	*inside the mountain*

5   Only one of these completed noun phrases contains two prepositions. Which one?

How did I do?

I can expand phrases with prepositions.

10: Linking clauses

In this unit you will learn
▶ to link clauses grammatically

Get started

Exam scripts handed in by students often contain sentences like this one.

I waited by the gates, I was feeling incredibly nervous.

The sentence contains two separate clauses. A clause is a part of a sentence that contains a verb. In this case, the first verb in the sentence tells you what the writer was doing. The second sentence provides information about the writer's emotions.

The two clauses are

I waited by the gates

I was feeling incredibly nervous

Practice

1 Write down each of the clauses in the following sentences.

He stopped suddenly, it was too late.

The passengers disembarked, the aircraft refuelled.

Each of the sentences looked at so far uses the same method of joining the clauses. This method is common but it is incorrect.

2 How are the clauses linked in each of the sentences?

Clauses can be separated into sentences of a single verb in length.

I waited by the gates. I was incredibly nervous.

Unlike the previous sentences, these sentences are correct grammatically. As well as being correct, single-clause sentences can be effective. Sometimes writers use them to create a tight and tense atmosphere.

3 Write out the following comma-spliced clauses as a series of three properly punctuated sentences.

He moved towards us, it was dark, I was scared.

Look at the single-clause sentences you have created. Notice how these sorts of sentences can sometimes be very effective.

As you have seen, single-clause sentences can *sometimes* be effective. On the whole, however, sentences need to be more than one clause in length and they need to be properly linked. They should not be joined (or *spliced*) with commas.

 Joining clauses together with commas is such a common mistake that examiners have a name for it. It is called **comma splicing**. (Splicing is a name originally given by sailors to different ways of joining ropes together in knots.) Texts that splice clauses with commas in this way are always penalised.

The most common way of joining up single clauses is by using connectives. Words used as connectives include

and   so   before   while   after   but   because   since   as   although

The most frequently used connective is *and*.

*The passengers disembarked **and** the aircraft refuelled.*

And is overused, however, and you should find alternatives whenever appropriate.

*The passengers disembarked **while** the aircraft refuelled.*

4 Identify the connectives in the following sentences.

I thought hard about it before I left.

They'll leave when they've had enough.

It's a real problem while it continues.

Notice the clauses on each side of the connectives you just picked out. See how they form two shorter sentences *embedded* in the longer sentence.

Revision booster

Clauses can change places within sentences to create different effects.
While the aircraft refuelled, the passengers disembarked.
The second clause and the connective from the original sentence have moved to the front of this new sentence.

5 Using this example as your guide, rewrite the three sentences from question 4 in the same way.

How did I do?

I can link clauses grammatically.   ☐

11: Using connectives

In this unit you will learn
▶ to connect simple sentences

Get started

A **simple sentence** contains a single verb. The verb is normally attached to a noun or pronoun that it is *about*.

Paula combed her hair.

The verb is *combed* and the person who does the combing is Paula. The sentence is *about* Paula so it is said that Paula is the **subject** of the sentence. The subject sometimes *does something* to another noun. In this case, Paula combed *her hair*. Her hair is the thing which has had something done to it and it is said to be the **object** of the sentence.

A simple sentence might contain just a verb.

Stop! Wait! Run!

It can contain a verb and an object.

Take that! Bring water. Stay calm.

It could contain a subject and a verb.

Paula drives. He rollerblades. Harry flies.

Or it can contain a subject, a verb and an object.

Paula drives buses. Isadora eats pilchards. I love it.

Practice

1 In the following simple sentences, identify the

a three subjects

b five verbs

c four objects

Think! Arun made tea. Harry flies planes. Have fun. I collect fossils.

Simple sentences are certainly grammatical. If they are overused, however, they will make writing dull.

Look at the following two simple sentences.

Alana left school. She started a business.

These are two perfectly grammatical sentences. They contain two subjects (*Alana* and *She*), two verbs (*left* and *started*) and two objects (*school* and *a business*). You can probably see, though, that too many sentences like this will very soon send a reader to sleep. These sorts of sentences are fine once or twice in a text to add variety. On the whole, however, simple sentences need to be developed into sentences with more than one verb.

The easiest way of doing this is to insert a **connective** like *and*.

*Alana left school **and** she started a business.*

Other words used as connectives are

but   when   if   because   while   until   unless   since   as   although

2   Using a different connective each time, link each of the following pairs of simple sentences.

Sid cooks dinner. His mum does it for him.

He makes the toast. His eggs are boiling.

He washes up. Nobody else will do it for him.

He cleans his teeth. He watches the television.

Simple sentences can also be connected by using **participles**. Participles, remember, are verb forms that can follow *has* and *is*. For example

ridden   smiled   done   brought   gone   (perfect participle)

riding   smiling   doing   bringing   going   (continuous participle)

Here are two simple sentences.

Robin Hood rode to Nottingham. He prepared for the fight.

They can be linked with the word *having* plus the perfect participle.

***Having ridden** to Nottingham, Robin Hood prepared for the fight.*

Or the word *after* plus the continuous participle.

***After riding** to Nottingham, Robin Hood prepared for the fight.*

3   Using the sentences about Robin Hood as your guide, link these three pairs of simple sentences using the

a   perfect participles

b   continuous participles

The president waved to the crowds. He returned to his office.

He beat the egg. He poured it into the mixer.

Kirsty spoke to the press. She went back to her hotel.

How did I do?

I can connect simple sentences.   ✔ ☐

12: Combining clauses

In this unit you will learn
> to combine clauses

Get started

Recall that a **clause** is a part of a sentence that contains a verb. Writers can choose to produce single-clause sentences that look like these.

He howled in pain.

She drove the car.

It has snowed during the night.

I was happy at last.

You have finished it.

Steve agreed with her.

Practice

1 Identify the verb used in each of the single-clause sentences above. Remember that a verb can consist of a single word or a combination of words.

Remember also that single-clause sentences are only effective up to a point. All texts need sentences of more than one verb to create variety and depth. Verbs within sentences can be combined with the use of connectives. Look at this example.

Steve agreed with her. He understood her problem.

These two single-clause sentences could be combined in the following way with a connective.

Steve agreed with her because *he understood her problem.*

Of course, other connectives (such as *since, as soon as, when*) could be used to do the same job. Notice that the connective allows the writer to create a longer, more sophisticated sentence out of the pair of linked clauses.

Here are some more words used as connectives.

until   while   so   and   but   whenever   although   after

2 Look at the following pairs of clauses. Identify the connective that joins them in each case.

a The baby cried whenever he was put down in his cot.

b You must be careful or there could be trouble.

c He waited but they never arrived.

d You should go before they see you.

The continuous (or progressive) participle can also be used as a means of linking clauses. (The continuous participle is created by adding *ing* to the verb infinitive.) This is a very effective method, which you should use occasionally as a striking way of creating sentence variety.

Understanding her problem, Steve agreed with her.

3 Combine the following pairs of sentences, using continuous participles.

a Andre walked home. He felt miserable.

b The tears rolled down her cheeks. She laughed at her own joke.

c Everest is the world's highest mountain. It soars nearly 9000 metres into the sky.

> The past (or perfect) participle can also be used to link sentences. (The past participle is the form of the verb that follows *have/has* or *had* in the perfect tenses.)
>
> *This series has become very popular. It began only recently.*
>
> *Begun only recently, this series has become very popular.*
>
> **4** Combine the following pairs of sentences using the past participle as in the example above.
>
> a The centre has been a success. It was completed last year.
>
> b These mushrooms are delicious. They are cooked in butter.
>
> c This is a beautiful necklace. It is encrusted with rubies.

> ! A variety of well-combined clauses produces mature and stylishly written sentences.

Revision booster

For even greater variation, a participle phrase can sometimes be embedded after the first noun phrase in a sentence.

This necklace, encrusted with rubies, is beautiful.

Notice that the participle phrase embedded in the middle of the sentence is sectioned off with commas.

5 Rewrite the first two sentences from question 4 using the same method.

How did I do?

I can combine clauses. ☐

13: Phrases and clauses

In this unit you will learn
  ▶ to express detail concisely

Get started

Remember that a clause is a part of a sentence that contains a verb.

the man	is a noun phrase without a verb
the man in the film	is a pair of noun phrases linked by a preposition
the man walked	is a clause (because it includes a verb, *walked*)

Practice

❶ Which of the following are phrases (or pairs of phrases) and which are clauses?

a *some people at the stall*

b *she drives*

c *a couple*

d *the angry elephant roared*

e *my friend*

f *accidents happen*

Noun phrases can be made up of a single noun or pronoun. They can also be formed from clusters of determiners, adjectives and nouns.

it	(single pronoun)
Gabriel	(single noun)
that green parrot	(determiner + adjective + noun)
that green parrot with the blue wings	(two noun phrases linked by a preposition)

❷ Look back at the phrases and clauses in question 1 and identify a noun phrase made up of

a a pronoun

b a single noun

c a determiner plus an adjective plus a noun

3 Which of the phrases in question 1 consists of a pair of noun phrases joined by a preposition?

Extended noun phrases need to be used in sentences of more than a single clause. Look at the following example.

It was a beautiful tree. It produced colourful, sweet-scented blossom every year.

Both sentences contain extended noun phrases.

a beautiful tree and *colourful, sweet-scented blossom*

The detail is very good, but it could be expressed with greater economy. It could be more concise and more focused. This can be achieved by communicating the description in a single sentence.

It was a beautiful tree, which produced colourful, sweet-scented blossom every year.

Notice that *which* is used as a connective to join the two original sentences. It *refers back* to the tree that starts the description. For that reason, it is called a **relative pronoun**. Here is a list of the four common relative pronouns.

who   which   whose   that

Notice the following points. The connective *who* refers to people. The connective *whose* refers to something belonging to the original noun. The connectives *which* and *that* refer to things and are often interchangeable.

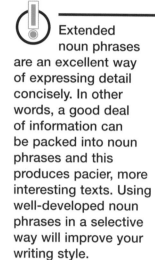 Extended noun phrases are an excellent way of expressing detail concisely. In other words, a good deal of information can be packed into noun phrases and this produces pacier, more interesting texts. Using well-developed noun phrases in a selective way will improve your writing style.

4 Join the following pairs of sentences using one of the connectives above. Use the example about the tree as your guide.

a *The old lady was a happy person. She made friends easily.*

b *It is a big problem. It causes lots of disagreements.*

c *Think about these people. Their lives have been changed.*

Revision booster

Increased variety can be achieved by embedding the second (or subordinate) clause within the main clause.

The old lady, who made friends easily, was a happy person.

5 Join the following pair of short sentences using an appropriate connective. Then embed the subordinate clause within the main clause following the example above.

The alien was a thoughtful being. He always helped others.

How did I do?

I know how to express detail concisely. ✔ ☐

31

14: Using adjectives

Get started

Adjectives are used to provide variety, detail and additional information about nouns.

Remember that nouns can combine into phrases with other sorts of words.

Nouns can sit by themselves before and after verbs.

Drink **water**.

They can link with determiners to create different meanings.

Drink **some water**.

Drink **your water**.

They can join with determiners, prepositions and other nouns to add further detail.

Drink **the water from the farm**.

Drink **this water in the cup**.

Another way of adding interest, information and variety to a noun is by using **adjectives**. Adjectives describe nouns.

Drink this **delicious** water.

Drink the **clear** water from the stream.

The adjectives *delicious* and *clear* provide extra information about the noun *water*.

You can normally identify an adjective by putting it in front of either the word *stuff* or the word *thing*. If the phrase sounds right, then you can be almost certain the word you are testing is an adjective. If it does not, then the word probably belongs to a different group.

Practice

1 Use the *stuff* and *thing* test to identify the five adjectives in the following list.

wonderful   sadness   absolutely   great   toad   brilliant   television   funny madly   warm

You might have noticed that words like *this, that, some, the, a, your, my* and *her* all look like adjectives using the *stuff* and *thing* test. Words like these are called **determiners** and they are very similar indeed to adjectives.

2 In the left-hand column on the following page is a list of determiners and adjectives. Match each of them with the appropriate noun in the right-hand column to make six new noun phrases.

Some overripe	clown
An aggressive	dog
My painful	glass
The shattered	hooligan
A painted	bruise
Your barking	grapes

3 Now add your own determiners and adjectives to the following nouns to make six new noun phrases like the ones you created above.

snake   fisherman   trees   Martian   fire   caves

There are many types of adjectives that tell readers different things about nouns. Adjectives can describe such things as

colour	*red yellow green*
shape	*oval square round*
size	*small gigantic tiny*
appearance	*old beautiful ugly*
mood	*angry happy sad*

4 Add at least one more word to each of the adjective categories above. If you get stuck, use a thesaurus. To do this, look up any of the words in the list and you'll find a set of words that are similar in meaning. Alternatively, if you can access a computer, right click on the word and go to *synonyms*. Using a thesaurus is a great way to improve your vocabulary.

 Use a thesaurus (or go to *synonyms* on a word processor) to find unusual and interesting adjectives.

The following passage demonstrates the need for adjectives. It is well written but would improve with more descriptive detail.

> The doctor slammed the door. He strode towards me and pushed his face into mine. I could see his eyes level with my own. I noticed on his jacket a streak of blood.

Important nouns here include   *doctor   face   eyes   jacket*

The doctor's emotional state should be clear to you.

5 a Add mood adjectives to the first three of these nouns to give the reader extra detail about the doctor's temper.

b Add a colour adjective to *jacket* that will contrast with the (red) streak of blood and therefore highlight it.

c Now rewrite the passage.

How did I do?

I know how to use adjectives for variety and detail.   ☐

15: Using adverbs

Get started

Adverbs are normally found giving extra detail to verbs. A lot of them end in the letters *ly*.

walked **angrily**   *laughed* **harshly**   *waved* **happily**

These adverbs tell the reader *how* something was done. They add extra detail to the verb in an efficient and accurate way.

Notice that the adverbs *angrily*, *harshly* and *happily* are related to the adjectives *angry*, *harsh* and *happy*. In fact, we could keep the meaning of the above phrases by replacing the adverbs with the adjectives.

walked **in an angry way**   *laughed* **in a harsh way**   *waved* **in a happy way**

Practice

1 Choose a single adverb to add to each of the following verbs. Your aim is to tell the reader more about *how* each action is performed.

shouted   ate   scribbled

It is common for adverbs to end in the letters *ly*. There are many that don't, however. Look at the following list of sentences.

I am working **hard**.

I will work **tomorrow**.

I **sometimes** *work*.

I **almost** *worked* **yesterday**.

I **always** *work* **here**.

Adverbs can come either before or after the verb. In this case the verb is *work*. Each of the adverbs in these five sentences tells the reader more about the action of *work*.

2 Here are five more adverbs. Include them in five short sentences like the ones above. Use a different verb for each of your sentences and start each sentence with *I*.

nearly   well   now   never   there

Sometimes you will see adverbs in pairs. In this case, the first adverb is giving information to the second.

*The work is **sometimes properly** done.*

The adverb *sometimes* is being used to give detail to, or modify, the adverb *properly*.

Sometimes you will see adverbs modifying adjectives.

*The work is **often brilliant**.*

The adverb *often* is used to give the reader information about the adjective *brilliant*.

Sometimes, adverbs are used to modify a whole sentence.

***Incredibly**, the lightning missed the tree.*

***Astonishingly**, I managed to finish.*

> ! Adverbs can also give detail to other adverbs, adjectives and whole sentences.

Look at the following sentence.

Her clothes are tidily folded.

The adverb *tidily* can be modified with a new adverb so that the sentence would read

*Her clothes are **sometimes** tidily folded.*

3

a Write two more sentences like the one above that use an adverb to modify *tidily*.

b Now write sentences of your own that start with the following adverbs. Separate the adverb from the rest of your sentence with a comma.

   Astoundingly,   Sadly,   Hopefully,

Revision booster

There are various tests for identifying an adverb. Remember that as with the tests for nouns and adjectives, there will always be exceptions. But the following rule holds true most of the time. *An adverb will make sense if you put it either before or after the word* done *in the following sentence:* It is done.

4 Use this rule to identify the adverbs in the following list.

excellently   hold   damage   almost   frequently   thoughtful   just now   stay   coolness

How did I do?

I can employ adverbs accurately.   ✔ ☐

16: Verbs and adverbs

In this unit you will learn
- ▶ to use verbs and adverbs imaginatively

Get started

The words you use have a very big impact on the quality of your writing. Choose your words carefully and your writing will improve.

Read these sentences.

Fazillah *looked* at the picture.

She *glanced* at the picture.

She *examined* the picture.

She *peeked* at the picture.

The second word in each of these sentences is a verb. It tells us what Fazillah was doing. Each verb tells us that Fazillah looked at the picture but that she did it in a slightly different way each time.

We can explain the effect of verbs like this.

She *peeked* at the picture suggests she took a very quick look at it. It also suggests that maybe, for some reason, she shouldn't be looking at it.

Practice

1. Explain the effect of the verbs used in the second and third sentences.

2. Make four new sentences from the one below by changing only the verb *walked.*

   Adelina walked to the door.

   If you get stuck, use a thesaurus. Locate the word *walk* and you will find a list of words that are similar but have slightly different meanings. If you have a computer, right click on *walk,* go to *synonyms* and then to *thesaurus.*

3. Now compare your four sentences based on *Adelina walked to the door.* Explain the effect of the verbs used in two of your sentences.

Look at this sentence about a ghost.

The ghost *moved* through the old house.

It gives us information about what the ghost did but it does not create an interesting impression. Changing the verb can create a more interesting effect.

The ghost *drifted* through the old house.

4 Change the verbs in these sentences to create interesting effects.

The dragon *flew* into the air.

Ewan *ate* his chocolate cake.

The army was *beaten*.

 Using verbs imaginatively is fun to do and makes your writing much more varied.

Adverbs can be just as effective as verbs in making what you write more interesting.

Fazillah looked at the picture.

might be made much more effective in the following ways:

Fazillah looked at the picture *angrily*.

She looked *carefully* at the picture.

She *quietly* looked at the picture.

As a rule, adverbs add interest and detail to verbs. In each of the sentences about Fazillah she looks at the picture in slightly different ways. Notice that the adverbs in the examples all end in *ly*. This is the case with many adverbs, but not all of them.

5 See if you can add three new adverbs to the following sentence.

Adelina walked to the door.

Revision booster

6 Change a verb, add an adverb, or do both, to add interest to the following sentences.

The king *rode* into battle with his knights.
He *hit* his rival with a battleaxe.
His enemy *fell* to the ground.
Arrows *went* past the king's ears.
He *said* to his soldiers, 'Enough! No more!'
The king and his warriors *went* to their castle.

How did I do?

I can use verbs and adverbs imaginatively.   ✔ ☐

17: Spelling and sounds

In this unit you will learn
▶ to look at vowels and consonants in spelling

Get started

The **vowel** sounds in English are represented by the letters *a*, *e*, *i*, *o*, *u* and *y*. There are more sounds than there are letters, though, because we can make combinations that produce extra sounds.

For example *plan* produces a *short a* sound, and *plain* produces a *long a* sound. Say the words to yourself and you will hear the difference. The *long a* in *plain* takes longer to say than the *short a* in *plan*.

English (like all languages) has a number of vowel sounds, some of them short, some of them long.

Practice

1 Look at the following words. In each case, say whether the vowel sound is *short* or *long*. Don't look at the number of letters used to make up the vowel. Listen to the way it sounds when you read it to yourself.

slam   sleet   claim   rough   bet   print

Vowels are known as *open* sounds. This is because your mouth is *open* when you produce a vowel. The air comes straight out of your lungs and out of your mouth. The shape of your mouth changes to produce each different vowel.

Say each of the vowels (just the vowels) in the words above. Notice how the shape of your mouth changes as you pronounce each one differently.

Consonants are different. These are called *closed* or *stop* sounds. This is because they are produced in your mouth by *stopping* the air from your lungs and then pushing it out to produce a whole range of sounds.

Make a *d* sound, for example. Notice that your tongue goes up to the roof of your mouth (it stops the air) and then lets go suddenly to make the consonant sound. Now make a *p* sound. Instead of stopping the air with your tongue, this time it is stopped (and then let go) by your lips.

Words are made by combining vowels and consonants. For example, the word *add* is made by joining the open vowel sound *a* with the closed consonant sound *d*. Make the sound (say the word) to yourself to *feel* how this open and close system works.

2 Say the following consonants to yourself: *f g m t*. Describe which parts of your mouth are used to make each of them.

Understanding vowels and consonants is crucial to becoming a good speller. English spelling is complicated, but there are rules, and if you learn them your spelling will improve. For example, English has a rule that the letters *est* can be added to some adjectives to create the idea of *most*.

funny	*funniest*
small	*smallest*
blue	*bluest*
plain	*plainest*
thin	*thinnest*
green	*greenest*
big	*biggest*
true	*truest*
silly	*silliest*
fine	*finest*

The first word in each pair is called the **root** or **stem** word. The spelling of the second word in each of the pairs follows some simple rules. They are

a If the root ends in a long vowel and a consonant, just add *est*.

b If the root ends in a short vowel and a consonant, double the consonant before adding *est*.

c If the root ends in the vowel *e*, then drop the *e* before adding *est*.

d If the root ends in the vowel *y*, then drop the *y* and add *i* before adding *est*.

3 Which rule (a, b, c or d) is followed by each of the ten words in the list above?

A famous playwright once said that English spelling was so difficult that *fish* could be spelled *ghoti*. Take the *gh* sound from *enough*, the *o* sound from *women* and the *ti* sound from *motion* and you'll see what he meant. Actually, he was exaggerating. A *gh* never makes an *f* sound at the start of a word and a *ti* never makes a *sh* sound at the end. Understanding these sorts of rules, like the ones about adding *est*, will greatly help your own spelling.

Revision booster

4 Add *est* to the following roots, remembering the spelling rules you have learned.

free   great   fit   mad   tiny   bare   red   angry

How did I do?

I understand vowels and consonants in spelling. ☐

18: Spelling homophones

In this unit you will learn
▶ to spell common homophones

Get started

Homophones are words that *sound* the same as each other but which are spelled differently. For example

cereal   spelled in this way is something you eat   *but*

serial   spelled like this is a story told in separate parts

hair   spelled in this way is something you might comb   *but*

hare   spelled like this is an animal quite similar to a rabbit

Practice

1   Write down homophones for the following six words.

flour   waist   through   knight   right   piece

Now look at these words.

everywhere   here   somewhere   nowhere   where   there   anywhere

2   a   What concept do all these words refer to?

b   Which four letters appear at the ends of all these words?

Taken together, these two facts provide a useful spelling rule:

The common *place* words all end with *here*. Other words with a similar sound are spelled differently, and have different meanings.

here refers to a place   *hear* is what you do with your ears

where refers to a place   *wear* is what you do with clothes   *we're* is *we are*

there refers to a place   *their* is a determiner like *my* and *your*   *they're* is *they are*

The apostrophes should be easy to remember: if your meaning is *they are* or *we are* (or *it is, you are, there is*) then the spelling of that word is *they're* or *we're* (or *it's, you're, there's*).

Remember from previous units that determiners are words like *their*, *his*, *your* and *my*. They go before nouns like this.

their problem   ***my*** coat   ***his*** future   ***her*** suggestion

So something that *belongs to them* uses the determiner *their.*

3 Use the rules in this unit to correct the following mistakes.

Their driving over now.	*There not doing it properly.*
Hear comes the bus.	*Did he where a tie?*
He doesn't know wear it is.	*Sit over their.*
They like they're new house.	*Theirs a problem.*
I can't here you very well.	*The problem is there's.*

The homophones covered in this unit are often misspelled in tests. Make sure you know them well, so that you can use them even when you are under pressure.

It is very common for *its* and *it's* to be confused. Remember these rules.

The full spelling of *it's* is *it is*; *it's* uses an apostrophe to show that a letter has been removed (in this case *i*). It works in the same way as other words that have been shortened.

it is	becomes	*it's*
there is	becomes	*there's*
here is	becomes	*here's*

If you can replace *it's* in a sentence with *it is*, then you know you have used it correctly.

Its without an apostrophe is a determiner that defines a noun, just like *their.*

For example, *You shouldn't judge a book by **its** cover.*

4 Are the following uses of *its/it's* correct or incorrect?

Its a beautiful day today.

The team has lost it's best player.

I think that its too far to walk.

The snake shed it's skin.

How did I do?

I can spell common homophones.

19: Spelling errors (1)

> In this unit you will learn
> ▶ to spell commonly confused words

Get started

The same spelling errors often appear repeatedly in the work of quite different students. There is normally a good reason (and a clear explanation) when so many students continue to make the same mistakes.

One of the most common errors is for students to spell *have* as *of*. The reason for this is that in daily conversation, most people hear abbreviated words like *could've, might've* and *should've* in sentences like

*They **should've** done more to help.*

If you read these abbreviated words out to yourself, the *'ve* part sounds just like *of*. This leads people to write things like

*I could **of** done more.*

This is *always* an error. You can see from the original form that the *'ve* abbreviation comes from the word *have*. So, when you mean *have*, write *have* not *of*.

*I could **have** done more.*

Practice

1 Read the following sentences. Which word is correct in each case: *of* or *have*?

a *I could **have/of** eaten all the cakes.*

b *Which **have/of** the cakes do you like?*

c *She might **have/of** bought the cakes.*

In many parts of the country, the word *are* is pronounced the same as *our*. As a result, the two words are sometimes confused. There is no need for this. The word *are* describes the state of things. The word *our* is a determiner that shows something belongs to a group of people. Look at the following examples.

*You **are** old*	Describes the state of being old.
***Our** house is in the middle of the town*	The house belongs to a group of people.

If you name something that belongs to a group of people then use *our*.

2 Read the following sentences. Which word is correct in each case: *are* or *our*?

a *I think **are/our** problem is that we **are/our** too cruel.*

b *Is it true that they **are/our** coming to **are/our** party next week?*

c *I think that are/our products **are/our** the finest on the market.*

Sometimes spelling errors result from two words being mistakenly joined. There are two very common examples of this. The first results from the combination of the separate words *a* and *lot*. The phrase *a lot* is usually used as an adverbial phrase to mean something like *to a great extent*. Here is an example.

He has changed **a lot** *recently.*

Many words that *seem* something like the phrase *a lot* are spelled as a single word.

about   around   appear   anew   alike

However, *a lot* is always made up of two separate words.

To confuse matters, there is a pretty rare verb *allot* which means to give a share of something. This has created a noun, *allotment,* which describes the place where people can grow their own plants. Unless you are in the unusual position of writing about this sort of thing, keep the phrase *a lot* as two separate words.

Another adverbial phrase, *in fact,* often suffers the same fate as *a lot.* The two separate words that make up the phrase are mistakenly joined. *In fact* is often used in the same way as *indeed.* This is the source of the problem. Look at this example.

This is not much good. **In fact**, *it's totally useless.*
This is not much good. **Indeed**, *it's totally useless.*

Indeed is one of a big group of words that begin with the letters *in.* Others are

insight   instead   insist   infer   into

In fact is not one of this enormous group of words. Keep the two parts of the phrase separate.

The more you understand about language the better your spelling will be.

3

In each of these sentences there are either one or two common mistakes. Identify them and write out each word as it should be spelled. There are ten mistakes in all.

He should of come to us. I think are family would have looked after him well.

There are alot of people coming tomorrow. Infact, there are loads of people coming.

Do you think are school will have a new pool?

The weather will of improved by next week. It seems to be getting better now, infact.

Is are sports centre going to close or are we going to keep it?

It would of been better if we could of taken the car to our garage.

How did I do?

I know how to spell commonly confused words. □

20: Spelling errors (2)

In this unit you will learn
- ▶ to spell commonly confused words

Get started

Often words are misspelled because they become confused with other words. Perhaps the most common example of this is in the two high frequency words *quite* and *quiet.* Looking at the grammar of these words will help to pull them apart.

- *quite* is an adverb that means something like the adverb *fairly.* It normally suggests that although something isn't brilliant, it isn't bad either.

  The new software is quite *good.*

- *quiet* is an adjective that describes a noun.

  It was a very quiet *evening by the sea.*

- *quietly* is an adverb that describes the action of doing something without noise.

  He whispered quietly *to himself in the corner.*

Practice

1 Read the following sentences. Identify the correct choice of word in each case.

a The mouse was extremely *quite/quiet/quietly.*

b He wanted to have a *quite/quiet/quietly* day by the sea.

c The wind whispered *quite/quiet/quietly* in the trees.

d The road is *quite/quiet/quietly* a long way from the track.

e It's going to be *quite/quiet/quietly* a long time before then.

Your knowledge of grammar can also help you with another commonly misspelled word, *already.* This is an adverb that means something has happened.

I have already *spoken to her.*

Already is one of a group of words that begins with the letters *al.*

although   almost   altogether   alright   always

These words can *never* be spelled in the following ways.

allready   allthough   allmost   alltogether   allright   allways

Sometimes the word *all* can be used before words like *ready* and *right* and *ways*. When it is used like this it means *every* or *everyone* or *everything*.

Is the team all *ready?*   *Is everyone ready?*

Are the fireworks all *ready?*   *Is everything ready?*

Are all *ways blocked?*   *Is every way blocked?*

Notice, though, that the word *all* remains separate from the word that follows it.

The following pairs of words are very often confused.

practice/practise   device/devise   advice/advise

The first word in each pair (the one with the letter *c*) is an abstract noun. The second word in each pair (the one with the letter *s*) is a verb. You can *hear* the difference in the second two pairs. The noun is used to describe a thing.

My *advice* is to go to the gym.

With enough *practice* you will improve.

The verb is used to describe the act of doing something.

I *practised* for hours.

She is *advising* him on his finances.

He *devises* ways of improving road safety.

He will *practise* until he gets better.

2 The following sentences contain some of the common mistakes looked at in this unit. Locate each error and write down the corrected version. You should be able to find ten mistakes in all.

He practices the guitar for allmost all of his spare time.

All though it is quite by the river it is still fairly busy.

My advise to anyone in this business is to be ready for anything.

Is the building allready complete? They've worked quiet quickly on it.

The buildings are already. They worked on them for allmost a year.

Allthough it's a long way away, we arrived quite early.

How did I do?

I know how to spell commonly confused words.

21: Vowel length

In this unit you will learn
▶ to investigate vowels in spelling

Get started

Long vowel sounds in English are spelled in different ways.

Practice

The long **a** vowel sound can be spelled in many ways including the following.

ai as in p**ai**n and tr**ai**n

ay as in p**ay** and tr**ay**

a-e as in p**age** and st**age**

eigh as in **eigh**t

1 Write down one more example of each of these spellings of the long **a** sound.

The long **e** vowel sound can be spelled in some of the following ways.

ee as in m**ee**t and f**ee**d

ea as in m**ea**t and tr**ea**t

ie as in ch**ie**f

The long **i** vowel sound is usually spelled

igh as in n**igh**t and fl**igh**t

y as in m**y** and fl**y**

i-e as in m**ine** and sw**ine**

2 Write down one more example of each of these spellings of the long **e** and long **i** sounds.

The long **o** vowel sound is mainly spelled

ow as in fl**ow** and gr**ow**

o-e as in st**one** and dr**one**

oa as in m**oa**n and r**oa**d

The long **u** vowel sound is usually spelled

ew as in fl**ew** and n**ew**

u-e as in t**une** and br**ute**

oo as in m**oo**n and s**oo**n

3 Write down one more example of each of these spellings of the long **o** and long **u** sounds.

The **short** vowel sounds are

a as in c**a**t and h**a**t

e as in b**e**d and h**ea**d

i as in h**i**t and kn**i**t

o as in r**o**b and c**o**st

u as in c**u**t and s**o**n

Short vowels are spoken in the space of a single tap. Long vowels are not.

Say the short and long vowel sounds to yourself. Make sure you can hear the difference.

Each of the following 30 words contains the letter **c** followed by one or more vowels.

*acid   incensed   raincoat   recite   coast   carrot   excitable   receive
economy   calendar   centre   city   costly   accuse   incite   incurable
cotton   custard   catalogue   company   reception   cable   cinema   case
ceiling   current   decay   deceit   honeycomb   accumulate*

The vowel sounds that follow the letter **c** in each case are either short or long **a**, **e**, **i**, **o** or **u**.

4 Make ten groups of three words each, according to the vowel sound after the letter **c**. Remember that your groups are based on the sound of the vowel, not the spelling.

The letter **c** can be pronounced **hard** as in **c**at or **soft** as in **c**ity.

5 Look at the groups you have made.

a Which vowel sounds following the **c** create a soft **c** sound?

b What do you notice about the spelling of the long **e** sound when it comes after a **c**?

Sometimes we add suffixes to change the meanings of words. For example

fit is a base word which can be turned into fit**ter** fitt**est** fitt**ing** fitt**ed**

light is a base word that can be turned into light**er** light**est** light**ing** light**ed**

The **t** in **fit** is doubled because the vowel before it is short.

The **t** in **light** is left alone because the vowel before it is long.

6 Remember this spelling rule and add two of the above suffixes (**er**, **est**, **ing**, **ed**) to each of these words.

green   hold   spin   soon   gun   dread

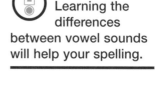

Learning the differences between vowel sounds will help your spelling.

How did I do?

I can investigate vowels in spelling.   ✔ ☐

22: Spelling suffixes

In this unit you will learn
▶ to join suffixes to stems using regular patterns

Get started

Suffixes are regularly occurring word endings like *ly, ness, ful, ment, er* and *est.* The same suffixes normally do the same thing to the words they join. For example, the suffix *ness* normally turns an adjective into a noun.

sad sadness   mad madness   good goodness   happy happiness

The **stem** (or **root**) is the word that's there before the suffix is added. For example, the suffix *ing* can be added to the following stems.

look looking   stay staying   become becoming   crave craving

Practice

1 Add the suffix *ful* the following stem words.

   hope   sorrow   beauty   pain   success

2 What happens to a final *y* when the suffix *ful* is added?

   Hope, sorrow, beauty and so on, are all abstract nouns.

3 What does adding the suffix *ful* do to an abstract noun?

4 a Now add the suffix *ly* to the five words you created in question 1.

   b What is the effect of adding this suffix?

5 a Add the suffixes *ed* and *ing* to the following stems.

      pick   race   dry   oblige   apply

   b What happens to a final *e* when these suffixes are added?

   c What happens to a final *y* when the suffix *ed* is added?

The suffixes *ible* and *able* cause many spelling difficulties. Words ending in these suffixes are adjectives such as

incredible   indestructible   terrible   edible

and

valuable   disposable   traceable   manageable

Learn some basic rules for adding suffixes and your spelling will improve.

6 Look back at the words *valuable* and *disposable*.

a What are the stem words of these adjectives?

b What has happened to the final *e* of the stem word in each case?

Now look at the words *traceable* and *manageable*.

The *e* has not been dropped from the stem in either case. This is so that the *c* in *traceable* and the *g* in *manageable* stay soft. The following spellings are incorrect because they would make the consonants hard. You may be able to 'hear' that the spellings are wrong.

tracable   managable

The same applies to similar pairings like

notice   noticeable   damage   damageable

If you are in doubt as to whether you need to use *ible* or *able* then remember this useful rule. If you are *able* to do something with the stem then the suffix is likely to be *able.* For example

I am *able* to *like* something so the adjective is *likable.*

I am not able to *respons* something so the adjective is *responsible.*

7 Now add either *ible* or *able* to the following 'stems', remembering the rules you have learned.

poss   break   love   horr   respect   slice

How did I do?

I know how to join suffixes to stems using regular patterns.

✔
☐

23: Making plurals

In this unit you will learn
▶ to pluralise nouns

Get started

The plural form of a noun is used when more than one thing is referred to.

For example

The book on the table | The **books** in the library

The child in the car | The **children** in the nursery

The witch on the broom | The **witches** round the cauldron

Singular nouns are made plural in a number of different ways.

The most common and simple way to make a plural is to add an *s* to a noun.

apple – apples   dragon – dragons   picnic – picnics   invitation – invitations

But *es* is added if the noun ends in the following ways: *ch, s, sh, ss* or *x*.

batch – batches   bus – buses   bush – bushes   kiss – kisses   fox – foxes

Practice

1 Make the following nouns plural.

fire   match   mess   mission   box   plantation   flash   television

If a noun ends in a consonant + *y* then it is pluralised by changing the *y* to *ies*.

daisy – daisies   bunny – bunnies   puppy – puppies   lady – ladies

But if a noun ends in a vowel + *y* it is pluralised by adding an *s*.

donkey – donkeys   trolley – trolleys   Friday – Fridays

Nouns ending in *f* or *fe* can be pluralised either with *ves* or *s*. You can normally hear the difference if you say the words to yourself. Try it with the words below.

loaf – loaves   wife – wives   knife – knives   belief – beliefs   giraffe – giraffes

Plural spellings of three nouns ending in *f* are worth memorising. These are *scarf – scarfs* or *scarves*
roof – roofs or *rooves*
hoof – hoofs or *hooves*

2 Now pluralise these nouns.

pansy   life   play   caddy   cliff   leaf   osprey   reef

If a noun ends in the vowel *o* then it is normally made plural by adding *es*.

tomato – tomatoes   potato – potatoes   mango – mangoes

A few words that have come into the English language more recently simply add an *s*.

casino – casinos   disco – discos   yo-yo – yo-yos

Sometimes nouns are made plural by changing the vowels within them.

tooth – teeth   man – men   mouse – mice   woman – women

3 Pluralise the nouns in the following sentences.

The man looked after the goose.

His tooth came out in the potato.

The woman played with the yo-yo.

The tomato outlasted the mango.

The mouse went to the disco.

Some nouns are called uncountable. Such nouns cannot usually be turned into plurals. Examples are

sugar   bread   coffee   milk   butter   water   blood   sand

We don't normally talk about *breads,* for example, unless we are thinking about specialist breads from around the world.

We pluralise an uncountable noun by putting a countable noun in front of it and pluralising that. For example

one loaf of bread   becomes   *two loaves of bread*   not   *two breads*

one drop of blood   becomes   *two drops of blood*   not   *two bloods*

4 Pluralise the nouns *sugar, coffee, milk, butter* and *sand* by placing a new noun before each of them and pluralising that.

How did I do?

I know how to pluralise nouns.   ✔ ☐

24: Writing speech

Get started

Writers often use **direct speech** in fiction as follows. In printed texts you will often see single speech marks used rather than the double speech marks (or quotation marks) in this unit. In handwritten work, use double speech marks.

> The miller returned home, exhausted.
>
> "How did you do?" asked his wife.
>
> "Not well," he replied. "The market was bad today."
>
> He hung his coat on the peg and trod wearily up the stairs.

Notice that you need to begin a new paragraph whenever anyone starts or stops speaking.

Practice

1 Punctuate the following passage, using *exactly* the same layout as in the example above.

> The doctor went back to her surgery. Where have you been asked her secretary. I went to the chemist to get some pills replied the doctor. I have a bad headache. She took off her coat and walked into her office.

Direct speech (the speech included *inside* the quotation marks) must be separated from the rest of the text by either a comma, a question mark, an exclamation mark or a full stop.

If a full stop is used inside the closing speech mark, then it's time to start a new paragraph. A small letter is used in text that continues on from a question mark or an exclamation mark.

2 Use speech marks and any other necessary punctuation to correct the following sentences.

Stop he shouted I want to get off

What's the problem she asked

It's a good painting said Maisie why don't you hang it on the wall

Direct speech is extremely effective used in isolation to create a sort of punchline or conclusion that rounds something off neatly. Here is an example of this from a famous folk tale.

> The Emperor walked proudly down the golden streets. The crowds gasped in wonder at his majesty and splendour. He turned into the courtyard and gave one last imperial wave.
>
> "He's not wearing any clothes!" cried a small boy in delight.

Use direct speech in fiction but use it sparingly. When it is overused, writing can become difficult to follow and may lack detail and depth.

Indirect speech (sometimes called **reported speech**) is used to summarise in a writer's own words what has been said. It is, as its alternative name suggests, often used in writing that reports events.

The President walked into the room and told the press that there was no alternative but to ban the use of cars.

This sort of speech has no need for any special punctuation. The effect of using this way of reporting speech can be seen by setting the text out as direct speech.

The President walked into the room. The press fell silent.

"There is no alternative but to ban the use of cars," he said.

You can see that reporting speech makes it more matter of fact.

The extract about the miller and his wife can be turned into reported speech like this.

> The miller returned home, exhausted. His wife asked him how well he had done. He replied that he hadn't done very well because the market was bad. He hung his coat on the peg and trod wearily up the stairs.

❸ Turn the passage about the doctor and her secretary in question 1 into reported speech. Use the passage about the miller and his wife as a guide.

How did I do?

I can use direct and indirect speech. ✔ ☐

25: Punctuating speech

In this unit you will learn
▶ to punctuate speech correctly

Get started

All sorts of writing can benefit from the use of direct speech. It is important to make sure that if you include speech in your writing then you do it correctly.

Speech marks (or inverted commas or quotation marks) look like this ("...").

They are wrapped around the words that a person is quoted as speaking.

Speech can follow your own text.

Carmen said, "Come to the factory with me."

Carmen asked, "Would you like to come to the factory?"

Carmen screeched, "Come to the factory!"

Use a comma to separate the speech from your own text.

Begin the speech itself with a capital letter. Put the end stops (full stop, question mark, exclamation mark) inside the speech marks.

Your own text can follow speech.

"Stay away from me," said Feri.

"Can I have an ice cream?" asked Feri.

"Stop it!" shouted Feri.

There must be some punctuation inside the closing speech marks. This can be a comma or a question mark or an exclamation mark. It must not be a full stop.

Your own text can be between two sentences.

"Stay away from me," said Feri. "I have flu."

"Can I have an ice cream?" asked Feri. "There's a shop over there."

"Stop it!" shouted Feri. "You're tickling me."

> Using direct speech can add variety and interest to your writing.

Practice

1 Add speech marks to the following sentences. Add capital letters, commas, question marks, exclamation marks and full stops where necessary.

a *do you like apples asked Maddox they're my favourite fruit*

b *Amber shouted stop*

c *is it muddy asked the trooper*

d *go shouted the excited driver behind me what are you waiting for*

e *my cousin is coming tonight he replied*

Start a new line when a new speaker begins to talk. Begin another new line when you return to your own text. Use the following sample as your guide.

The car drove silently along the deserted beach. It came to a halt, its engine cut, its headlights dimmed. The two cops lay hidden behind a dune.

"What's going on?" whispered McClary.

"I have no idea," replied Bergen. "Why don't you wait and see?"

The two men remained quietly watching.

2 Add the necessary punctuation to the following text. Start new lines when you need to.

Amelia and Ollie walked quickly to the edge of the cliff. Is this where it happened asked Ollie. I don't know replied Amelia. But I think it was somewhere round here. The two of them walked briskly on.

In printed texts you will often see single speech marks rather than the double speech marks studied in this unit. In handwritten work, use double speech marks. Save the single ones for the following situations.

● When you want to quote speech within speech.

  "I think she said 'what a bore' but I couldn't quite hear her," said Tom.

● When you want to show you don't really believe something.

  He's always having these 'pains' in his foot.

● When you need to handwrite the name of a book, a film, a play and so on.

  "We're going to see 'Pirates of the Caribbean' tonight," replied Shilla.

3 Write your own sentence with single quote marks within double speech marks.

How did I do?

I know how to punctuate speech correctly. ✔ ☐

55

26: Commas in action

Get started

Sometimes, commas are used in the wrong places. Often, commas are not used when they're needed. This unit will help you use commas accurately in your own writing.

Commas are needed in lists of adjectives and nouns.

● *It's the most foolish, ridiculous, harebrained idea I've ever heard.* (adjectives)

● *I need ropes, nets, hooks, wires and floats.* (nouns)

Don't put a comma between the last adjective and the noun in a list of adjectives.

Don't put a comma between the last noun and the connective *and* in a list of nouns.

Practice

1 Add commas where necessary to the following list of adjectives and nouns.

a This is the warmest sunniest driest summer on record.

b The suppliers sent apples bananas pears grapes mangoes and oranges.

Commas are used to separate your own text from direct speech.

The robot said, "Come with me."

"I prefer skateboarding," replied Ronnie.

If your own text comes first, put the comma outside the speech marks.

If the direct speech comes first, put the comma inside the speech marks.

2 Add commas where necessary to punctuate the following sentences.

a Ashley groaned "My feet are aching."

b "Take him away" said the spiteful prince.

Commas are needed to mark off phrases that give us more information about a noun.

Clark Kent, better known as Superman, has been around for many years.

Anjie Rice, businesswoman supreme, is back on the circuit.

Elvis Presley, 'the King' to his fans, is still making news.

Notice that these sorts of sentence still make sense if the descriptive phrase is removed.

 Used properly, commas provide good balance and structure to sentences.

3 Add commas where necessary to separate the main nouns in the following sentences from their descriptive phrases.

a The Sears Tower once the world's tallest building dominates Chicago.

b Dogs our best friends evolved from wolves.

c Jenna my cousin is a farmer.

Commas are often wrongly used in place of full stops or connectives.

Read the following.

I smiled at the baby. She looked at me.

There are two separate things going on here and they are represented by the two verbs *smiled* and *looked*. They are separated (properly) by a full stop. The two sentences could also be joined by any of a number of connectives to make

I smiled at the baby and/when/because she looked at me.

Separating sentences with a full stop or joining them with connectives is fine. What must not happen is for these sorts of sentences to be joined with a comma.

I smiled at the baby, she looked at me.

This is called **comma splicing** and is responsible for many lost marks in tests and exams.

4 All the following sentences have been wrongly spliced (joined) with a comma. Replace the comma with a connective to make a properly punctuated sentence. Choose from the following list of connectives if you like, although there are lots of alternatives.

and   while/whilst   but   as   though   when   because

a I don't want to go to the post office, there's always a queue.

b I was working on the computer, the virus struck.

c I listened to the noise from next door, it deafened me.

d The rabbit leapt from the hat, the magician smiled.

e Bananas are my favourite fruit, I've never liked apples.

f I couldn't do it, I tried very hard.

How did I do?

I can use commas accurately.

✔
☐

27: Using apostrophes

In this unit you will learn
▶ to use apostrophes correctly

Get started

Apostrophes are used to show **possession** or to indicate that **abbreviation** (shortening or omission) has occurred. Follow the simple rules in this unit and avoid the many mistakes made by students in this area of their writing.

Like many languages, English makes use of phrases like

the quality of the material   the colour of the bus   the thorns on the bush

Writers in English can also show possession in a second way.

the material's quality   the bus's colour   the bush's thorns

An apostrophe and an *s* is added to the very end of the noun that does the possessing. *The material,* for example, possesses *the quality,* not the other way around.

Practice

1 Change the following phrases using an apostrophe and an *s*.

the roar of the tiger   the scent of the flower   the broom of the witch

 ——————
Possessive pronouns ending in *s* do not take apostrophes. These are *yours, his, hers, its, ours* and *theirs*. For example

The book is Rahul's. It is his.

The magazine is Jamilla's. It is hers.

All the serious reading is theirs.

The comic is yours.
——————

When a plural noun ends in the letter *s,* all that should be added to show possession is an apostrophe.

the prey of the tigers   the scent of the flowers   the cauldron of the witches

become

the tigers' prey   the flowers' scent   the witches' cauldron

2 Change the following phrases in the same way as in question 1.

the shrieking of the parrots   the value of the jewels   the destination of the boxes

Apostrophes of abbreviation are used to show when parts of words have been left out, especially in speech. In natural spoken English, most people, most of the time, do not say the whole of phrases like

*we would like   she had better   the fire is out   It is raining
I could not possibly*

These phrases can be written out as they are spoken, with an apostrophe to show where a letter or letters have been left out.

we'd like   she'd better   the fire's out   It's raining   I couldn't possibly

3   Add an apostrophe and shorten the following phrases where appropriate.

a   he is driving

b   they are laughing

c   I do not like it

d   we should not

e   they must not

Notice that the abbreviated forms of *will not* and *shall not* are *won't* and *shan't*.

Apostrophes of abbreviation are features of informal English. Only use them when you are sure you want to create an informal atmosphere.

Phrases such as

could have   might have   would have

are abbreviated in people's speech to make

could've   might've   would've

Listen to your own speech and that of others and you will hear this. Because the 've abbreviation sounds like *of*, many students then write the abbreviated forms as

could of   would of   might of

This is *never* right.

An apostrophe of abbreviation is used when *it is* or *it has* is shortened to *it's*.

Its (with no apostrophe) is a different word that shows possession. For example

The government changed its policy.

The bird built its nest.

Remember *it's* for abbreviation and *its* for possession.

4   Put apostrophes into the following sentences if they are necessary.

a   *The casino finally closed its doors.*

b   *Its been a wonderful place.*

c   *I think its tremendous the way its always been open.*

d   *Its problem was a lack of customers.*

How did I do?

I can use apostrophes correctly.

28: Foregrounds in sentences

In this unit you will learn
- ▶ to foreground for variety

Get started

Remember that simple sentences are those that contain just a single verb. Here is a string of three simple sentences.

Saul strode to the force field. He put out his hand. He disappeared in an instant.

⊕ **Words, phrases and clauses can all be foregrounded. They are normally separated from the rest of their sentences by a comma.**

This piece of writing is grammatically correct but it is dull. One way of adding variety is by altering the sentence structure. The sentence structure can be altered by something called **foregrounding**. Writers foreground when they put something unexpected at the beginning of a sentence. For example, the three sentences above all start with *Saul* or *He*. To add variety you could foreground the adverbial phrase at the end of the third sentence. The adverbial phrase is *in an instant*.

Saul strode to the force field. He put out his hand. In an instant, he disappeared.

This is an improvement on the original. Notice that the foregrounded adverbial phrase is separated from the rest of the sentence by a comma.

Practice

1 The three sentences below all contain adverbial phrases. Rewrite them so that the phrases are foregrounded. Do not forget to include the comma.

He'll be coming in a second.

She strode off in a fury.

He lay down silently on a lonely hilltop.

Single-word adverbs can also be effective in a foregrounded position.

Angrily, Saul strode to the force field.

2 Add single adverbs as foregrounds to the following sentences. Remember the comma.

They parted for the last time.

The children ran into the fairground.

A complex sentence contains two or more verbs. Clauses are those parts of complex sentences that contain verbs. For example, the sentence

Saul strode to the force field as the humming grew louder.

contains two clauses based on the verbs *strode* and *grew*.

Saul strode to the force field

the humming grew louder

Notice that these two clauses could form two separate simple sentences with one verb each. The two clauses in the complex sentence are joined by the connective *as*. The second clause can be foregrounded to create variety in just the same way as you foregrounded the adverbial phrases and the single adverbs.

As the humming grew louder, Saul strode towards the force field.

3 Foreground the second clause in each of the following three sentences. Again, don't forget to include the comma.

I'm going to lose my temper if you don't stop messing around.

It was a real problem when she found out.

Take care until the next time.

Participle phrases can also be foregrounded as in the following examples.

Saul shuffled towards the force field, grumbling irritably.

Grumbling irritably, Saul shuffled towards the force field.

4 Foreground the participle phrases in these sentences. These already need commas, to make the phrase refer to the subject of the sentence.

He watched the film, laughing all the time.

The baby woke me, crying loudly.

She prepared her performance, breathing deeply.

Revision booster

Using the techniques learned in this unit, the original three sentences could be reformed in a much more interesting way.

Looking determined, Saul strode to the force field. Bravely, he put out his hand. In an instant, he disappeared.

5 What different features have been foregrounded in each of these three sentences?

How did I do?

I can foreground for variety.

29: Sentence expansion

In this unit you will learn
▶ to develop verbs and use connectives

Get started

Writing in good sentences is one of the foundations of success in English. You need to understand how to identify and use verbs before you can write successful sentences.

A verb is a 'doing' word. It tells us about actions. Here are three verbs.

walk   *read*   *play*

We can combine each of these verbs with other types of words to make short sentences.

I *walk* home.

She *reads* comics.

Stephan *plays* basketball.

Practice

1 Write three different sentences of your own using the verbs from the list above.

2 Now make three new sentences using each of the following three verbs. Make each sentence no more than three or four words long.

drive   *have*   *make*

Look back at the three sentences formed at the start of this unit.

Each of these sentences can be made more detailed by telling the reader something extra about an action.

I walk *slowly* home.

She reads comics *every day*.

Stephan plays basketball *at the gym*.

3 Take the sentences you wrote in question 1 and add detail to them as in the examples above.

Sentences that contain only one verb are called **simple**. A simple sentence can be quite long, but if it contains only one verb it is still called simple.

I walk slowly home *with my noisy friends.*

She reads comics every day *before breakfast.*

Stephan plays basketball at the gym *round the corner.*

4 Take the sentences you wrote in question 2 and see if you can make them longer as in the examples above. Keep each of your sentences simple: do not add other verbs to them.

If we add verbs to the verbs already in a sentence we can include even more information.

We can add extra verbs to sentences by using **connectives**. These are also known as **conjunctions** or **bridge words**. Examples are

and	*when*
but	*if*
so	*whether*
because	*while*
or	*until*

They help writers to bolt together sentences like this.

I *walk* home. I *have* my dinner.

I walk home *and* I have my dinner.

She reads comics *because* she likes them.

Stephan plays basketball *but* he finds it hard work.

5 Look back at your sentences from questions 1 and 2. Add a connective and a second verb to make six completely new sentences. Try to vary the connectives you choose.

Well-written sentences help readers understand exactly what you want to say.

How did I do?

I can develop verbs and use connectives. ☐ ✔

30: Synonyms for effect

In this unit you will learn
▶ to select verbs for effect

Get started

Read the following passage. It is a section of persuasive writing about the use of seatbelts on coaches.

> I think that all passengers on coaches should be made to wear seatbelts. I think that many lives would be saved if this were to happen. I think it very important that this suggestion should become law.

This is a well-structured piece of writing except for its over reliance on the verb *think.*

Practice

1 How many times is the verb *think* used in this short extract?

A verb like *think* can, of course, be used once in a text like this. If it is repeated, though, it will sound repetitive. This statement is *almost* always true. There are exceptions (in really passionate speeches, for example) where a verb can be repeated almost endlessly.

If you have come across Martin Luther King's *I believe* speech you will have seen how this can work. However, in your own writing it is best to avoid this sort of repetition unless you're absolutely certain of what you are doing.

2 Think of at least two verbs that could be used to replace *think* in the passage above. Then rewrite the passage with your new verbs. Notice how the style (and therefore the persuasiveness of the text) has improved.

! Using a thesaurus is a really excellent way of developing a mature and interesting vocabulary.

Thesauruses are extremely useful for the sorts of exercises in this unit. If you have a thesaurus, look up the word you want to replace. You will find a list of possible substitute words that have similar meanings. Only use those words you feel confident you understand.

If you use a word processor, you will almost certainly have a thesaurus in the software. The normal procedure is to right click on the word you want to replace and then follow the instructions.

A substitute word (that has a similar meaning to the word it is replacing) is called a **synonym**.

3 Use a thesaurus (or a word processor programme) to find three synonyms each for the following verbs.

a *speak*

b *talk*

c *shout*

Now read this passage from a work of fiction.

> Dawkins spoke furiously to his team mates and then walked away. He walked into the changing room, removed his boots and put them angrily on the floor. He was speaking quietly to himself when Forsyth noisily walked in.

Most of the verbs in this passage are in the simple past tense. Remember that this is the verb tense most commonly used to narrate and tell stories.

4 Find and write down the six verbs (one word in length) used in the simple past tense.

The passage is well written and creates good effects. The choice of verbs, however, is not so good. One verb is repeated three times and the others might have been chosen to create better effects.

For example, the verb *removed* suggests something being done carefully and quite calmly. Dawkins is clearly not in the mood to take his boots off like this. Choosing verbs like *ripped* or *pulled* (with the preposition *off*) would have helped the effect enormously.

*Dawkins **ripped off** his boots.*

5 Write down synonyms that replace all the simple past tense verbs you have just identified. Try to increase the effect of anger communicated by the scene. Choose a verb for Forsyth's entrance that shows him interrupting Dawkins' thoughts.

6 Which (two-word) verb in the last sentence is used in its past continuous form?

7 Replace the continuous participle with a different one that suggests quiet, muffled speech.

8 Now write out the whole passage with the verbs you have chosen to improve the effect. Notice how crucial verbs are in determining the atmosphere and impact of the text.

How did I do?

I can select verbs for effect. ☐ ✔

31: Paragraphs

In this unit you will learn
▶ to organise text into paragraphs

Get started

What are paragraphs? Paragraphs are chunks of writing. Each chunk is about a separate thing. Writing that is properly paragraphed is easier to read because it is clear and planned.

Organised paragraphs are forgotten when writing is not planned. Here is an example.

> My favourite animal is a crocodile. Crocodiles are cold blooded and can stay still for a very long time. There's an extremely large crocodile at Paignton Zoo. Crocodiles are native to many countries including Australia. Some people keep them as pets. Crocodiles are predators, which means they hunt live prey. They are mainly a sort of light green in colour. They do not have live young like mammals but lay eggs. They drag their victims under water and kill them not with their teeth but by drowning. Their eyes are near the tops of their heads. Lots of crocodiles live in African rivers.

This may all be true but it is unplanned and unclear. The paragraph contains scrambled information about crocodiles

● as reptiles

● in captivity

● worldwide

● as predators

● to look at

Practice

1. Start to tidy up the scramble by picking out two sentences from the crocodile paragraph for each of the five topics in the list above. For example

As reptiles   *Crocodiles are cold blooded and can stay still for a very long time.*

As a result of tidying up this sentence jumble you now have a very good paragraph plan. Your plan has five separate sections, which can be used as five separate paragraphs. You have two sentences already for each of those paragraphs.

The paragraph about crocodiles 'to look at' could be developed like this.

> Crocodiles are mainly a sort of light green in colour. Sometimes, though, they are more a browny grey so that they can blend in with the muddy rivers and vegetation they lurk in. Their skins are knobbly and rough and they have rows of teeth as sharp as razors. Their legs are short, squat and powerful. Their eyes are near the tops of their heads so that they can see above the water without revealing their bodies.

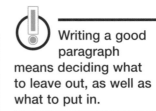

Writing a good paragraph means deciding what to leave out, as well as what to put in.

This a much better paragraph because the writer has written only about what crocodiles look like and nothing else.

2 Note down six separate things we learn about a crocodile's appearance.

The writer could have been tempted to write about crocodiles as predators but stuck well to the task of describing appearance. There are three phrases that relate crocodiles' appearance to the fact that they are predators. These add interest without altering the main point of the paragraph.

3 Write down the three phrases that mention crocodiles as predators.

4 Make a paragraph plan based on your own favourite animal. It could be a wild animal or a pet. Plan which four or five features of the animal you want to write about and then arrange those features into separate paragraphs.

Let's say, for example, you wanted to write about your pet cat. You could decide to separate your ideas into organised sections like this.

- My cat's appearance and what I like about it

- The way the cat hunts and what she enjoys doing outside

- The way my cat behaves around humans

- Unusual things my cat does

- My cat's attitude towards food

Now write your own plan based on the one above.

Revision booster

Choose one of the paragraph headings from the plan you made in question 4. Expand and develop this section into a full paragraph of about five or six sentences. Concentrate only on the subject mentioned in your heading. Use the paragraph about crocodiles' appearance as a guide.

How did I do?

I know how to organise texts into paragraphs.

32: Language analysis

In this unit you will learn
▶ to analyse a piece of writing

Get started

Mrs Thrimble is an extremely tidy lady and her most prized possession is her word drawer. In this drawer, tucked away in a corner of the kitchen, is her collection of words and phrases, all neatly organised. Unfortunately for Mrs Thrimble, a family of mischievous text rats live beneath her floorboards. Every night, after dark, these rats scrabble into the word drawer and rearrange all the words and phrases into texts. You can just imagine how annoying it is for Mrs Thrimble, every morning, to have to tidy her words and phrases away again.

Here is a text that poor Mrs Thrimble found written by the rats not long ago.

> We love the forest. We really do! The splendid green flowers sprout from the soil. The mighty old trees tower above. Who could feel anything but joy to see such a beautiful place? We dance and we play while the leaves swish above. We are freer than air as we run through the woods. We are the luckiest rats alive, there's no doubt of that.

Practice

Mrs Thrimble was most annoyed to find this text because the rats had used some of her favourite words and phrases. See if you can help her tidy them back into the drawer.

The first thing the text rats have stolen is a pronoun they use to describe themselves. They use the pronoun to start no fewer than four of their sentences.

1 What is the pronoun and how many of them have the rats taken?

Mrs Thrimble is very fond of the following sentence pattern.

pronoun + verb + determiner + noun

She thinks it is a simple and direct way to express an idea.

2 a Find a four-word sentence in the passage written by the text rats that follows this pattern.

   b Now write out a sentence of your own for Mrs Thrimble that follows the same pattern.

3 a Which adverb have the rats used in the second sentence to express how much they love the forest?

   b How else does this sentence express the strength of their love?

Mrs Thrimble likes alliteration in descriptive writing as long as it's not used too much. She remembers her teacher telling her that alliteration is the prominent use of a consonant sound (like *d*) within a short stretch of writing.

Look at the techniques used in good writing and use them in your own texts.

④ Which three words in the third sentence of their text have the rats used for alliteration?

Mrs Thrimble also likes imaginative verbs in descriptive writing, just so long as they're not overused.

⑤ The text rats took three of her least used verbs for use in their third, fourth and sixth sentences. Write them down.

Another technique Mrs Thrimble is very fond of is the use of rhetorical questions to appeal directly to the reader. Readers obviously can't answer these questions but they are a very useful way for writers to involve readers directly in a text.

⑥ Which rhetorical question have the rats taken from Mrs Thrimble's drawer?

Mrs Thrimble likes to see connectives used to join clauses within a sentence. One of her favourite connectives is *while.*

⑦ Which two clauses have the rats separated with this connective?

In the seventh sentence, the first clause is

We are freer than air

⑧ Write down the connective (a single word) and then the second clause in this sentence.

Mrs Thrimble is very fond of her adjectives.

⑨ Write down five adjectives used by the rats that describe either the flowers, the trees or the forest in general.

Adjectives can usually be changed by adding the **suffixes** *er* and *est.*

long longer longest   red redder reddest   silly sillier silliest

They show how the adjective relates to other things.

The freezer is *colder* than the fridge.   This bull is the *biggest* of the herd.

⑩ Help Mrs Thrimble to find one adjective to which the rats have added *er* and one to which they have added *est.*

How did I do?

I know how to analyse a piece of writing.   ✔ ☐

33: Grammatical features

In this unit you will learn
> to comment on grammatical features in texts

Get started

Jamal is a fourteen-year-old from Manchester who keeps a regular diary. This is an extract from one of his entries, written after a visit to his local surgery. His doctor believes he has an infection and Jamal has gone for a blood test.

Miss school this morning. That's the good news. Why do I miss school? I have to go to the surgery for a blood test. That's the bad news. Actually … that's the very, very bad news …

Arrive at the surgery. My sweet mother is as usual very loud and very embarrassing. Why does the entire waiting room have to know that I am a) having a blood test and b) suffering pains when I urinate? It seems to me that both these things are private and yet not everyone appears to share this view.

The receptionist calls my name. Everyone looks at me as if to say – 'he's the one who can't wee properly'. I retain my dignity as well as I can and stride (though my legs are wobbling) to the nurse. She asks me all sorts of questions ('where does it hurt' and 'how exactly does it feel') before sticking the needle in.

Practice

1 a What is the purpose of Jamal's visit to the surgery?

   b Why does Jamal seem quite pleased at the start of the extract?

   c Who seems not to share Jamal's view that his problems are private?

Many sentences in English follow the pattern: noun + verb + noun. For example

I made cocoa.

Hermione ate worms.

When writers use informal English (or when they are making notes) they sometimes leave out the first noun. It can add to the sense that the reader is part of the experience and doesn't need to have everything spelled out.

Made cocoa and put up the tent.

Ate worms and went to bed.

2 Write out the two sentences in which Jamal leaves out the noun before the verb.

The difference between the present and past tense in English is quite easy to recognise.

The receptionist calls my name.   is present tense

The receptionist called my name.   is past tense

3 Which tense does Jamal use in his account?

The present tense is sometimes used to describe accounts and events that took place in the past. It is another method of creating informality.

Read Jamal's entry to yourself but add the two missing pronouns at the start of the sentences and change the whole thing into the past tense. The first sentence would be *I missed school this morning.* Notice that it seems less chatty and more formal.

In the last paragraph, Jamal says he is trying hard to retain his dignity.

4 a Explain why Jamal feels his dignity is under threat.

   b What verb does he use to describe the way he tries to walk to the nurse?

   c What attitude does he want to show the rest of the waiting room by walking in this way?

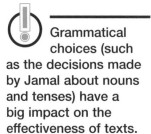

Look again at this sentence from the end of the first paragraph.

Actually ... that's the very, very bad news ...

Jamal uses this sentence to emphasise how bad he feels about his visit to the surgery.

The adverb *actually* refers back to the previous sentence. It shows that the previous sentence wasn't strong enough.

5 How does Jamal make his new sentence stronger?

Revision booster

6 Use the adverb *actually* in your own informal writing to perform the same task as in Jamal's account. Complete the following sentences.

I don't like oysters. Actually ...
It was funny. Actually ...
I don't seem to remember it. Actually ...

How did I do?

I can comment on grammatical features in texts. ☐

In this unit you will learn
> to retrieve information

Get started

Read this description of Earth written by a visiting alien.

> Planet Earth is a moderately fertile world covered mainly in water. Temperatures vary but would generally be either too hot or too cold for our farmers to grow crops. The land in the hot areas is sandy and in the cold areas it is often covered in ice. There are some significant mountains, the largest of which is around 9000 metres in height. These areas, like those that are too hot and too cold, would obviously be of little interest to us.
>
> There are some areas where the soil is fertile and the climate is temperate. These places are usually at around sea level. There are enough regions like this on Earth to make colonisation worth our while.
>
> At present, there are a number of life forms existing on the planet. Some appear not to move, being rooted to the ground, rather like the plants we grow as crops. Others are rather large, with long necks, great teeth or extraordinarily long noses. There is also a rather strange animal that seems to dominate the planet, at least in terms of the noise it makes. It lives, not in caves or trees or rivers, but in oversized buildings that it makes for itself. It also appears to communicate using something like language. It is, however, a rather puny and weak-looking creature which we would have little difficulty in clearing aside should we wish to.

Practice

1 a What does the alien say that most of the Earth is covered in?

b How high does the alien say the highest mountain is?

c At what height are most of the fertile and temperate regions?

Remember that noun phrases are single nouns or words that cluster around a noun and modify it. *Earth* is a noun phrase and so is *Planet Earth*.

Writers can communicate lots of detailed information in single noun phrases.

2 a Which (four-word) noun phrase used after *Planet Earth* describes it in more detail?

b Name the determiner, the adverb, the adjective and the noun that make up the phrase.

c Which (four-word) noun phrase is used to describe human beings?

3 Noun references are chains of meaning that link texts together. In the second paragraph, the noun *areas* is used. Which other two nouns, used soon afterwards, link up with the noun *areas*?

Sometimes readers can use quotations from a text to support their understanding of what has been read. For example, if you wanted to identify the alien's attitude towards humans, you could express it like this.

The alien describes them as 'rather puny and weak-looking'.

4 Now look at the way the alien describes animals such as giraffes, tigers, crocodiles and elephants. Locate the section that suggests the alien has seen these animals and express the information as a quotation. Set your sentence out in the same way as the extract about humans above and begin with

The alien describes them as ...

5 Look through the first paragraph and find adverbs that express the following ideas. The adverbs are in the same order they appear in the text and the first one is done for you.

neither fertile nor infertile   *moderately*

on the whole the Earth is covered in water

in general

covered in ice for most of the time

it is obvious

Remember that adverbs often (but not always) end in *ly* and that you can check for an adverb using the *it is done* test.

Revision booster

Look at the start of the third paragraph.

6 What adverb could the alien have used instead of the phrase *At present*?

Adverbs can modify adjectives, prepositions and other adverbs as well as verbs.

7 Which adverb (similar to *quite*) is used four times in the third paragraph, once before a preposition and three times before adjectives?

How did I do?

I can retrieve information. ☐ ✔

35: Alphabetical texts

In this unit you will learn
▶ to alphabetise and use a dictionary

Get started

Dictionaries are used so that word meanings can be found and spellings can be checked. Words in a dictionary are listed in a very strict order that never changes. So, to use a dictionary properly you must know how to use the alphabet.

To find the word *sequence* in a dictionary, you need to look at the first letter, which is **s**. This means that it will be grouped with all the other words in the dictionary that begin with **s**. It will be in the group after all the words beginning with **r** and before all those beginning with **t**. This is because of the order of the letters **r s t** in our alphabet.

Practice

1 Put the following ten words into the order you would find them in a dictionary.

weight	*material*
believe	*fierce*
audience	*remember*
jealous	*tomorrow*
separate	*daughter*

Look at this list of words, then read the hints that follow.

sob

so

rye

soak

snug

● **r** comes before **s** in the alphabet.

● If you can't sort words by the first letter, use the second, third or fourth letter.

● The second letter of *snug* is **n**. **n** comes before **o** in the alphabet.

● Sometimes a complete word is the same as the first letters of another, longer word. When this happens, the short word is placed before the other, longer word or words.

● The third letter of *soak* is **a**. **a** comes before **b** in the alphabet.

2 Write the five words out in alphabetical order.

Now look at this group of words.

heath	*gym*
hear	*heat*
gyrate	*heather*
funny	*happiness*
he	*fun*

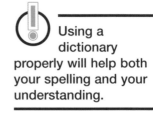

Using a dictionary properly will help both your spelling and your understanding.

3 Explain why

a *fun* must come before *funny*

b *fun* and *funny* must come before all the other words

c *happiness* must come before *he*

4 Now put the whole list in its proper order.

5 Put this list of words beginning with **p** into alphabetical order. When you have done this, find each of them in a dictionary.

punnet	*putrid*
pullet	*puggaree*
purloin	*puce*
punkah	*pukka*
pugilist	*pug*

Revision booster

Spellcheckers on computers are very helpful but do not replace your own brain. Four of the words in the 'p' list in question 5 are not recognised by most spellcheckers and if you ran an autocorrect, the replacement spellings would actually be new (wrong) words.

If you have access to a computer, check the software dictionary meanings of the words in the list. How close are they to the definitions you found in your own dictionary? Then run a spellcheck. See how the autocorrected spellings are actually new, unrelated words that will make no sense if you allow them to be inserted.

How did I do?

I can alphabetise and use a dictionary.

36: Presenting information

In this unit you will learn

▶ to consider ways of presenting information

Get started

Read the following text.

The problem with science is that it often goes against common sense.

Example: You are sitting in a dinghy floating on the surface of a pool. Next to you is a heavy bag of stones. You throw this bag of stones into the water and it sinks to the bottom. Question: does the level of the water in the pool go up or down? Answer: it goes down. That doesn't seem right to me but apparently it's true.

How does a cube of ice make water colder? Now that one must be easy. The coldness of the ice obviously flows out into the water and makes it cold. Right? My scientific friends say not. The warmth of the water actually flows into the ice. In other words, the ice draws in the warmth rather than the water drawing in the cold.

Another one? Since we are talking about water, let's try this. How many molecules are there in a typical glass of water? No prizes for guessing. The number of molecules in a single glass of water is greater than the number of glasses of water in all the oceans. Or at least, that is what I'm told. No wonder science is so hard to believe.

Practice

1 a What does the writer feel is the main problem with science?

   b How many examples of science's strange conclusions does the writer come up with?

Writers often present information so as to highlight it. If separate pieces of information are kept apart in texts then everything is much easier to understand.

2 a How does the writer separate her examples from one another in the text?

   b In which two places are there separate sentences on the difficulties of science?

   c What is the purpose of the first of these sentences?

Look at the last sentence of the second paragraph of the text.

That doesn't seem right to me but apparently it's true.

This is the first sentence in which we find out that the writer does not have expert knowledge of the information she is presenting.

3 a What is it that doesn't seem right?

   b What phrase could the writer have used in place of *apparently*?

   c What does the writer show the reader with her use of the word *apparently*?

4 The writer uses two other complete sentences to show that others have more scientific knowledge than she has. Write them down.

5 Find the sentence containing the word *obviously*.

   a Who is it obvious to that the coldness of the ice flows out?

   b Is this obvious conclusion correct?

   c How does this sentence support the main idea?

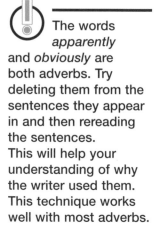 The words *apparently* and *obviously* are both adverbs. Try deleting them from the sentences they appear in and then rereading the sentences. This will help your understanding of why the writer used them. This technique works well with most adverbs.

The writer uses very short questions in her text.

6 Write down the two shortest questions.

Short questions create a feeling of chattiness. This in turn helps to create the sense of a relaxed and informal text.

7 Why might the writer have wanted to make this particular text informal?

The writer seems to direct questions straight at the reader in order to make the reader feel more involved in the text. Another way she does this is through her use of the pronouns *you* and *we*.

8 a What does the writer ask the reader to imagine by using the pronoun *you*?

   b What does the writer ask the reader to imagine with the pronoun *we*?

Revision booster

The writer uses an informal style throughout the passage. One part of this style is her use of single nouns before a colon. This is what it looks like.

Conclusion: I'm staying put.

9 Which three words does the writer place before a colon in this way?

How did I do?

I can consider ways of presenting information. ☐

37: Structuring information

In this unit you will learn
▶ to assess informative prose

Get started

Read the following extract from a passage about Tyrannosaurus.

> The name Tyrannosaurus, from ancient Greek, means tyrant lizard. Most people nowadays refer to this great dinosaur more simply as T Rex. This extraordinary beast has captured our imagination perhaps more than any other animal that has walked the Earth. It was a true giant. Its head was the size of a fully grown human. It stood as high as a double decker bus. But it is its reputation as a fearful predator which has held us in awe since its discovery over one hundred years ago.

Remember that a noun phrase is a group of words used together to refer to a noun. Noun phrases can be on their own, or they can be linked with prepositions. Look at the following examples.

they	a pronoun
some people	a determiner combined with a noun
many people in the museum	two noun phrases joined with a preposition

Sometimes noun phrases are used in **apposition**. This means they are placed adjacent, usuallly sectioned off with commas. Look at the following sentences. They both contain noun phrases in apposition.

Our black dog, Hercules, came running up the path.

Caesar, the name of the Roman emperor, is the root of Kaiser and Tsar.

In these examples, the second noun phrase is used to give extra detail about the first noun phrase.

ⓘ Use appositional noun phrases in your own writing to provide detail and variety.

How did I do?

❶ Write down the two noun phrases used in apposition in the sentences above.

Notice that the second noun phrase in the pair needs to be sectioned off with commas.

❷ Write down the noun phrase used in apposition in the Tyrannosaurus passage.

When writers make reference to the same thing throughout a text it is often quite hard to avoid repetition of noun phrases. The original noun phrase can be replaced with a pronoun (like *she* or *he* or *it*) but the repetition of pronouns is also to be avoided.

The answer to this problem lies in the imaginative variation of noun phrases. *Different* noun phrases can be used to *refer* to more or less the same thing. A text that uses *varied noun reference* will hold together well and be interesting.

To make all this clearer, look again at the passage about Tyrannosaurus. The simplest way the writer could refer to this dinosaur is either by using the noun *Tyrannosaurus* or the pronoun *it*. A more interesting text, however, has been produced by using varied noun phrases. Here are two of them.

tyrant lizard   this great dinosaur

These two noun phrases refer to the same thing. Repetition has been avoided by using different noun phrases to do it.

As with all informative writing, the Tyrannosaurus passage provides facts.

3 What facts do we discover about the following two details?

a the language the word *Tyrannosaurus* comes from

b when Tyrannosaurus was first discovered

Facts about unfamiliar things can often be made clearer with the use of comparisons. For example, few people would be able to picture a Diplodocus' brain if it were expressed in metric terms. Everyone, however, can imagine the brain if it is described as a comparison.

A Diplodocus' brain was no larger than a human's clenched fist.

The Tyrannosaurus passage makes comparisons like this twice.

4 What are the head size and height of Tyrannosaurus compared to?

Revision booster

5 **Find as many noun phrases as you can in the extract that refer to Tyrannosaurus. Include the two noun phrases provided above. Only include noun phrases that refer to the animal itself. Do not include references to parts of its body.**

How did I do?

I know how to assess informative prose.

38: Reading for detail

In this unit you will learn
▶ to find and use detail in texts

Get started

A few years into the Second World War a soldier called Arnie Brenning was captured by enemy forces and taken to a prison camp. Like most prisoners, he was sometimes allowed to write short letters home. This is an extract from one of them.

> We had a massive discussion about horses last night. Some of us air our opinions very readily, I can tell you that. I had an attack of giggles when Jim started on about the Grand National. He whacked me on the mouth to shut me up. We all miss Liverpool, there's no doubt about it. Are we all coming home? I hope so, soon, I really do my love.

During wartime, censors read letters and other documents to make sure they contain nothing important or secret. This letter was passed by a censor. Prisoners of war often listen in to their guards' conversations and try to send home details of what they hear.

Practice

1 Imagine you were the person who censored this letter. Your commander has been highly suspicious of Arnie Brenning since he arrived at the camp. He asks you a number of questions about the letter's contents. Answer them fully.

   a What did the prisoner say he was discussing with his friends?

   b When exactly did the prisoner start giggling?

   c What does he say his friend did to him to stop his laughter?

   d Which city does the prisoner seem to come from?

   e Who do you think the prisoner was writing to? Why do you think this?

2 The prison commander remains watchful of Arnie Brenning and his companions. He asks you, as the censor of Brenning's letter, two further questions about the mood of the prisoners. Answer them, giving reasons for what you say.

   a Are the prisoners happy with each other?

   b Are Brenning and the others happy at the prison?

Although his censors always read them closely, the prison commander could never find anything wrong with Brenning's letters, and they continued to be sent home until the end of the war. What the commander didn't know was that Brenning had told his family he would encode secret information in his letters if he were captured.

In the letter you just read, he chose to string his message out along the fourth word in each sentence. Now you know this, you should be able to unravel his code.

! Don't miss
   details like the
censors did. Read texts
closely to get the most
out of them.

3 Start at the beginning of the first sentence. Count four words in. The fourth word is *massive.* That is the first word of the coded message. Now go to the beginning of the second sentence and count four words in. Keep doing this until you have Browning's complete message. Write his secret message out in full.

Arnie Brenning's family sometimes wrote him encoded messages as well. In the next letter, the code is again strung along one of the words in each sentence, but this time it is not the fourth one. Work out which word. You can do this by seeing if words make sense when they are put together. For example, if you write down every first word in each sentence you get: *there we we we* ... which doesn't make sense. Try using every second word and so on until you get a clear message.

4 When you find it, write it out.

> There was no singing this Christmas, Arnie. We have need for good news. We want to help our neighbours but how are we to do it? We do worry so. I think our problems may just be beginning. We have soldiers returning tired and injured. The men are done in with the fighting, all of them. I think, on balance, we would do better to surrender now and cut our losses. Politicians in their smart suits tell us to be patient but they're not the ones who suffer. The only way now is to give in. We want to stop. If we get too much more of this I think the country will collapse, truly I do. I feel you want the war to stop as well, don't you Arnie. They say 'out of courage comes victory.' I say, 'of course,' but out of courage comes misery and defeat as well. I think there is no reason to go on.

Arnie's wife, Sheena Brenning, cleverly gave the censors who received her letters the wrong impression of her mood.

5
a How do you think the censors would describe her mood?

b What sort of things does she pretend are creating her mood?

c Who does she pretend to criticise for the situation?

d Can you think why Sheena Brenning might try to trick the enemy in this way?

Revision booster

6 Write your own coded letter based on those written by the Brennings. Make your letter sound as natural as possible so that your secret message is 'camouflaged'. When you have written your message, find a reader who can decode it.

How did I do?

I can find and use detail in texts. ✔ ☐

In this unit you will learn
▶ to locate detail in texts

Get started

This passage is taken from the programme notes for a carnival and procession. The event took place not long ago in Northumberland.

> The carnival officially begins at noon in the town square beside the library. The procession will leave the town centre and will progress gradually towards the sports centre in the park behind Smith Street. By mid-afternoon, the procession will reach the park.

The ability to locate factual information in texts like this is an extremely important skill. You must read closely and extract the precise detail you need.

Practice

1 a What time does the carnival begin?

b Where exactly is the park?

c When will the procession reach the park?

Remember that the main job of the adverb is to modify a verb as in the following example.

The train moved slowly.

The adverb *slowly* provides information about the verb *moved*.

2 a Write down the adverb that modifies the verb *begins* in the procession text.

b Which adverb is used in the second sentence of the text?

c Which verb does it modify?

Adverbs can provide lots of variety in sentence structure. This is because they can frequently occupy different places within the sentence.

The train slowly moved.

Slowly, the train moved.

3 Look again at the first four words of the procession text. Alter the order of these four words by changing the position of the adverb. Use the two example sentences above to help you.

Recall that adverbial phrases are short phrases that do a similar job to adverbs. Look at the following example of this.

The performances ended simultaneously.

The performances ended at the same time.

The adverb and the adverbial phrase both give information about *when* the action of the verb took place.

In the procession passage, there are two adverbial phrases that provide information about when an action occurs. One of these is

by mid-afternoon

> ⓘ Adverbials, like adverbs, can tell a reader *how*, *where* and *when* an action occurs.

4 Which other (two-word) adverbial phrase tells the reader *when* an action occurs?

In the first sentence of the passage, there are two adverbial phrases that provide information about *where* the action of the verb *begins* takes place.

5 Write down the two adverbial phrases that tell the reader where this action occurs.

Adverbial phrases can often move around within sentences, just like adverbs, to create a range of effects.

6 Look again at the adverbial phrase in the final sentence of the procession passage. Rewrite the sentence by moving the adverbial phrase to the end.

Recall that verbs can be more than one word in length. This is normally the case with verbs that express future time. The most common method of expressing the future in English is to add the verb *will* before the infinitive of the main verb.

It rained yesterday. It's raining today. It will rain *tomorrow.*

7 Find three examples in the passage of future time being expressed in this way.

Revision booster

Future time, oddly enough, can sometimes be expressed with a present tense verb.

He starts *next week*.

8 Find a single example in the text of future time being expressed in this way.

How did I do?

✔

I know how to locate detail in texts. ☐

40: Narrative features (1)

In this unit you will learn
▸ to explore features of narrative

Get started

The following extract is from the start of a group diary. It was written by Year 7 students on their return from a weekend hiking in the Yorkshire Wolds.

> We woke up early. Tent 3 had collapsed during the night and its inhabitants (Jessica and Minette) were using it as a duvet. Mr Walters was already cooking breakfast in a far corner of the field but he seemed unhappy. After a while we could see why. The sausages were stuck to the bottom of the pan because, as Mr Walters insisted, our school's portable gas cooker was 'out of date'. We believed you, Mr Walters. In the end we all had toast and nobody minded at all.

Narrative writing typically progresses in a way that can easily be followed by the reader. This diary account was intended to be read by students, parents and others who would not necessarily have any background information about the events described. It needed to be clear and well organised.

An important way of organising this sort of narrative is through the use of adverbs and adverbial phrases that relate to time. These words and phrases include

next   now   after a while   during the night   in the end   already   later   early

Words and phrases like this are crucial in organising events in a reader's mind. They show progression from one thing to another.

Practice

1 Five of the eight adverbs/adverbial phrases in the list above can be found in the diary extract. Which are they?

Reread the passage but take out the adverbs and adverbial phrases you located. Notice how the extract loses its sense of time structure.

Adverbial phrases can often be replaced by single adverbs. For example

at the current time	can become	*currently*
all of a sudden	can become	*suddenly*
in an instant	can become	*instantly*

2 Look at the last adverbial phrase you picked out in question 1. What single adverb could replace it?

This sort of narrative is designed to be interesting to a wide range of readers. One of the ways of making a report or a diary account interesting is to include anecdotes. **Anecdotes** are short stories, often amusing, that people recall as experiences.

3 This extract has two anecdotes. What are the two separate anecdotes described by the students in their account?

Neither anecdote would be funny if it wasn't for the reactions of those involved.

4 a How is the first anecdote made amusing by what the girls do?

b How is the second anecdote made funny by the teacher's response?

Inverted commas are often used to show that something is to be questioned. For example

He said he was 'busy working late' but I wasn't sure what he was up to.

They said they were 'in an important meeting' but I had my own ideas about that.

5 a Write down the section in the passage that is enclosed by inverted commas.

b The students clearly don't believe what's in the inverted commas. What do you think they do believe?

The passage continues after the inverted commas in a teasing sort of way.

6 Write down a complete sentence that is obviously used to tease Mr Walters.

The anecdote about Mr Walters is an example of very gentle **irony**. At no point do the students say exactly what they think about the burnt sausages. They just suggest it through the inverted commas. In their teasing sentence they actually say the *opposite* of what they believe and yet the reader still gets the point they are making.

7 The irony comes to an end with a four-word phrase. The phrase makes it clear that the loss of the sausages didn't *really* matter to anyone. What is it?

How did I do?

I can explore features of narrative.   ✔
                                            ☐

41: Narrative features (2)

In this unit you will learn
▶ to evaluate narrative features

Get started

A group of Year 8 students from a North Essex school recently visited a local zoo as part of an environmental awareness fortnight. One of their assignments when they returned to school was to write an account of their visit. Here is an extract from one of them, written by Zoe.

> *After free time, we went up to the study centre. The Zoo is built on a number of hills which caused endless complaints from the 'less energetic' members of our party. On our way, we saw an incredible white tiger in a massive enclosure. It came right up to the glass and bared its teeth. Moving swiftly on, we soon arrived at our goal. Work beckoned.*

Practice

1 Zoe mentions one of the animals that she sees.

a Which animal does Zoe see?

b Which adjective does Zoe use to express her admiration for this animal?

c What does the animal do that Zoe finds a little worrying?

2 Many people are concerned that animals should be looked after properly in zoos. What *two* details suggest that this animal is not hemmed into a cage?

Accounts and diaries often make use of something called **euphemism**. Look at these examples of euphemism.

He wasn't very adult	can mean	*He was childish*
She had a little too much	can mean	*She was greedy*
It was rather loud	can mean	*It was a terrible noise*

Euphemisms are often a gentle joke made by the writer to the reader. You can often imagine the phrase *you know what I mean* after euphemisms. It is as if the writer makes a comment and then winks at the reader.

Writers sometimes give euphemisms inverted commas. This is so that less observant readers do not miss the meaning. In the passage, Zoe gives her euphemism inverted commas.

3 a What (two-word) phrase does Zoe use to describe certain people in her group?

b Which single adjective could she have used (much more rudely) instead?

Remember that **adverbial phrases** work in the same way as adverbs. They tell us things like *when* and *where* actions occur.

*We finally arrived **late in the day***.

*We became very exhausted **on our long journey***.

*The bread disappeared **in an instant***.

Adverbial phrases can often be replaced by a single-word adverb.

*The bread disappeared **instantly***.

Another feature shared by single adverbs and adverbial phrases is that they can occupy different places in a sentence.

***Late in the day**, we finally arrived.*

Zoe uses two adverbial phrases in her first three sentences. They refer to *when* and *where* things occur.

4   a Write down both the adverbial phrases. They are each three words long.

   b Where does Zoe choose to place these phrases in her sentences?

Passive sentences are often used in narrative. They look like this.

The road has been mended.

The grass was cut.

Those clothes were washed yesterday.

Notice that in each case the reader does not know *who* performed the action of the verb: who did the mending or the cutting or the washing. Writers use passive forms like this for different reasons. In narrative, it is often because it doesn't matter who did the job of the verb. For example, it doesn't matter which company mended the road. All that matters is that the job has been done.

In one of her comments about the zoo itself, Zoe uses the passive form.

5   a Write out the part of her sentence that uses the passive form.

   b Why does she use it here?

 Use passives when the thing that is done is more important than the person who did it.

How did I do?

I can evaluate narrative features.   ☐

42: Story structure

In this unit you will learn
▶ to structure a story

Get started

This unit outlines a five-step approach to make story-writing easier.

The first of the five steps is to write your **opening**. A good way to start a story is by describing a setting, the place where the action of your story is to begin.

The sun rose over the quiet park. A single bird sat on a leafless branch.

Practice

1 Write your own introduction to a story by describing a setting. Your opening should be around one or two sentences long, about the same length as the example above.

The second step is to **develop the plot**. In other words, something needs to happen.

A young man in a leather jacket limped through the gates. In his hand he held a book.

2 Add one or more sentences to your story that develop your plot. Remember that the point of this section is that something needs to happen in the setting you've created.

Your third section is called the **complication**. Something must now take place that will create a problem or a difficulty.

He suddenly slowed. The book slipped from his grasp and he sank to his knees.

3 Add sentences to your story that describe a complication, something that causes concern.

The fourth section is the **crisis**, where the complication (the third section) is developed.

From the shadows behind the trees, a woman appeared. She walked towards where the young man now lay. She bent down, picked up the book, and strode away.

4 Write your own fourth section. It should in some way develop the complication you created in your third section.

The final section is the **conclusion** or ending. It should round off what has been written in the earlier sections of the story but it need not supply the reader with any answers.

The park was once again silent.

⑤ Finish your own story by writing a one- or two-sentence conclusion.

This five-step structure can be used to help you with almost any story-writing task.

The short story put together using the step-by-step guide now looks like this.

> The sun rose over the quiet park. A single bird sat on a leafless branch. A young man in a leather jacket limped through the gates. In his hand he held a book. He suddenly slowed. The book slipped from his grasp and he sank to his knees. From the shadows behind the trees, a woman appeared. She walked towards where the young man now lay. She bent down, picked up the book, and strode away. The park was once again silent.

This story is fine as it is. It is full of possibilities and is interesting to read. It can, however, be developed by adding extra detail to any or all of its parts.

Detail can be added, for example, to the **opening** of the story.

> The sun rose over the quiet park and the wind blew gently through the wintry trees. The grass was covered with the lightest dusting of frost. A paper bag, lonely and forgotten, clung to the thorny bushes. A single bird sat, still as a stone statue, on a leafless branch.

⑥ Add extra detail to part or all of your own short story in the same way as in the example.

Revision booster

Here is a second story. It is very different to the first one but it was put together in the same way, using the five-step structure.

> The bedroom was full of screaming children. Wrapping paper littered the floor. Niall, whose birthday it was, jumped on the bed. He started bouncing up and down. There was a terrible crack and the bed collapsed beneath him. Niall lay in a heap of broken slats and bedclothes. 'Happy Birthday,' said his mother, as she opened the door.

⑦ Identify the sentences that make up each of the five steps in the structure.

How did I do?

I can structure a story.   ✔ ☐

43: Text structure

Get started

Imran Alazari was potholing with a team of cavers in Morocco when he was trapped by a rock fall. His account starts in the moments just before the rear of his tunnel collapsed.

> 10.42 The guys are behind me but I can hear the low murmur of their voices. It's comforting. I'm a way ahead of them with the steady light of the torch. Everything is going to plan. Everything is organised and tight. And then, crashing like a distant storm. The horror grips me. I know it's a rock fall. I'm on my knees and then unconscious.
>
> 11.03 I come round. My torch is gone and it's pitch black. I hear the blood throbbing in my ears. The dread of my isolation dawns on me. I touch the cold rock to give me a sense of reality. The rocks have come down, I'm cut off, I don't know what's happened to my friends and I may die. My hands are sweating but I'm as cold as the stone beside me.
>
> 12.17 There's this sound of scratching. I feel a surge of hope. Are they coming? Is there someone else alive? And then I hear a patter. Hope swaps places with despair and misery. It was just a rat, some rodent sharing my tiny space. I'm powerless. I can only wait. I'm sitting on the lifeless rock and my head is in my hands.
>
> 14.34 The faint music of voices! They're coming. I feel excitement but fear as well. What if they can't get through? And then something else. A chink of light which opens up in the blackness. It gets bigger and bigger, quickly now. I hear the rocks tumbling again but now I feel joy because it's a wall destroyed not a wall created. The sun starts to beam through. Through the rocks I see a human face. The tears stream down my cheeks.

Imran divides his account into four paragraphs. Each of them tells the reader something different. The first paragraph, for example, could be summarised like this:

Imran describes the way his sense of security turns to horror when the rocks collapse.

Practice

1 Write single sentences to summarise each of the other three paragraphs.

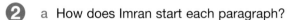

2 a How does Imran start each paragraph?

b Imran's timekeeping is precise. What might he be suggesting about the rest of his story?

c What do the endings of each paragraph have in common?

d What does the end of each paragraph stress to the reader?

> Decisions about structure (for example, starting each paragraph with the exact time of an event) can have a big impact on the effect of a text.

Once his torch had broken, the only light available to Imran came from his watch. This was not enough for him to see by and it was no use to him except for telling him the time.

3 a Note down four phrases in the text that relate to light and dark.

b How do these phrases help trace the progression of the story?

4 a Imagine you were in Imran's situation. Why would sound be so important to you?

b Find six more phrases in this extract that relate to sound and identify the different emotion or emotions that Imran links with each sound. For example

Quotation	Emotion
'... the low murmur of their voices.'	comfort

5 Look again at the table of Imran's feelings that you made as part of question 4. Draw a graph to show the ups and downs of Imran's emotions starting with the comfort and security he feels at the very beginning. Put time along the horizontal axis and emotion along the vertical axis.

Revision booster

Write your own imaginary account of a dramatic event. Use Imran's story as your guide. Write four short paragraphs and begin each of them with a reference to time.

How did I do?

I understand text structure.

✔
☐

44: Settings in fiction

In this unit you will learn
▶ to investigate setting in a classic text

Get started

In fiction, setting is extremely important. Writers spend a great deal of time and effort *setting the scene*. The scene is the background against which the story takes place. It is the stage on which the characters act.

Here are some examples of the way fictional setting is presented.

The heavy oak door creaked slowly open.

Happy Town is an absolute hive of busy activity.

The spaceship was a mass of buttons and flashing lights.

Setting can be a very reliable indicator of the kind of story you are reading.

Practice

1 What three types of fiction are the above settings taken from?

Of course, before long, a character must enter a setting, or the story will not be very interesting. The character will probably confirm what you thought about the setting.

The heavy oak door creaked slowly open and a stooping figure appeared.

However, the character and the action the writer puts into a setting can surprise us.

The heavy oak door creaked slowly open.

'I wish you'd oil this bleedin' thing,' said Mavis.

As you can see, the setting is therefore very important to a reader's understanding and enjoyment of a story.

The following extract is from a great short story by Arthur Conan Doyle called *The Speckled Band*. The story describes the adventures of Sherlock Holmes and his assistant Dr Watson as they try to solve a mysterious death. This part of the story is narrated (it is told) by Dr Watson.

> At Waterloo we were fortunate in catching a train for Leatherhead, where we hired a trap at the station inn and drove for three or four miles through the lovely Surrey lanes. It was a perfect day, with a bright sun and a few fleecy clouds in the heavens. The trees and the wayside hedges were just throwing out their first green shoots, and the air was full of the pleasant smell of the moist earth. To me at least there was a strange contrast between the sweet promise of the spring and the sinister quest upon which we were engaged. My companion sat in front of the trap, his arms folded, his hat pulled down over his eyes, and his chin sunk upon his breast, buried in the deepest thought. Suddenly, however, he started, tapped me on the shoulder, and pointed over the meadows.

Fiction often makes use of dramatic contrast. White stands out better against black than it does against beige. The same is true of contrasts in writing. The beauty of a mountain stands out if it is compared to a dirty old mine in the foothills. Think of the setting of the Fairy Godmother's factory in *Shrek 2*, if you have seen that film.

2 a What is Waterloo (a crowded London station) contrasted with in the first sentence of the Sherlock Holmes extract?

  b What 'strange contrast' does Watson himself comment on?

  c Watson loves the setting. How does this contrast with the reaction of his companion, Holmes?

Writers often use adjectives to help them describe a setting. They create descriptive noun phrases like

beautiful day

stunning views

wonderful scenery

3 Write down three noun phrases from the extract that indicate Watson's enjoyment of the setting.

Watson describes the perfect country setting.

4 a Write down four nouns used by Watson that are connected with the country.

  b Which noun used to describe the sky emphasises the perfection of the scene?

  c What season of the year is chosen for the setting?

  d What clue is the reader given about the season before it is directly mentioned?

The beauty of the scene described by Watson is emphasised by its abrupt ending.

5 What adverb, near the end of the passage, is used to bring the description of the countryside to an end?

How did I do?

I know how to investigate setting in a classic text. ☐ ✔

45: Figurative language

In this unit you will learn
▶ to work with figurative language

Get started

Figurative language is sometimes called imagery or poetic language. It is language designed to create a clear and immediate picture in a reader's mind. We might say to our friends, for example

It's cold.

But if we were reading a book, or writing some poetry, or watching a play or a film where the idea of *coldness* was being emphasised, we might find a more dramatic expression is suitable, such as

We walk in winter's icy grip.

There are many ways of using language figuratively. This unit looks at some of the important ones.

A very common and interesting sort of figurative language is **personification**. The above sentence about the winter makes use of it. Personification treats inanimate objects (things that aren't animals) as if they lived and breathed like us. In the real world, winter and the cold cannot *grip* anyone – the winter and the cold do not have hands or anything else to grip with. The writer just imagines they do to increase the dramatic effect.

Jack Frost has painted all the windows white.

This is the sort of personification you might get in a book for young children. The personification rests on the use of the proper noun (*Jack Frost*) and the verb (*paint*).

Practice

1 Look at the following sentences. Which word or words create the effect of personification in each case?

The sun has smiled upon us.

In the starlit sky the moon sat sadly.

The sea crashed angrily against the shore.

The tree went over like a falling giant.

Beyond the gate, the shadows seemed to dance and play in the fading light.

Personification is an excellent technique for you to use in your own creative writing.

Similes are a second important variety of figurative language. Similes are comparisons between one thing and another.

Her eyes were as green as emeralds.

His sense of humour was like a block of ice.

The lights spread along the shore like jewels on a chain.

Notice that the comparisons are introduced by the word *as* or *like*.

You might ask why writers compare things in these ways. They do it so that the description becomes clearer, more vivid, in a reader's mind. By comparing lights to jewels on a chain, for example, the writer provides a picture or an *image* of what the lights *actually look like*.

2   a   Match the phrases on the left with those on the right to produce five new similes.

The web was as delicate	like a bony hand.
His grating laugh	like an enraged giant.
The dead tree stood	was like an electric saw.
That night, the stars shone	as the finest lace.
The wind battered the glass	as bright as diamonds.

b   Which two of the objects in the left-hand column are *personified* by their simile?

Metaphors are the third variety of figurative language looked at in this unit. Metaphors are comparisons made without the use of the word *like* or *as*. Here are some examples.

Her eyes are sparkling emeralds.

You've been a safety net for me this year.

With their echolocation, these bats are flying submarines.

Notice that the writer could have chosen to use *like* or *as* to introduce the comparison in each of these three cases. Metaphors assume that the reader *understands* a comparison is being made without having to be told.

3

Each of the following is an example of either a simile, a metaphor or personification. Which is which?

The moon was a ghostly ship, plunging through a sea of clouds.

The moon shone out as bright as a searchlight.

The moon made its lonely way across the dark sky.

How did I do?

I know how to work with figurative language.

46: Descriptive language

In this unit you will learn
▶ to create impact with descriptive language

Get started

This is a poem written by an eleven-year-old from Inverness.

The Angry Stone

The stone is polished and bright
Like a dark brown eye
That stares and glares at me.

It lies alone on the table
Unhappy at being pulled from the beach
Where it has lain for a million years.

Before you start to write poetry you should remind yourself of some important facts.

● Writing poems is difficult to get right first time – you need to draft and redraft.
● Poems do not need to rhyme.
● Poems do not need to tell a complete story.

Practice

Poems are not organised into paragraphs like other sorts of writing. They are organised into stanzas.

1 How many stanzas are there in *The Angry Stone?*

Lines of poetry are not organised like those in other sorts of writing either. They are organised to create the maximum impact. If *The Angry Stone* were written out in normal English it would lose a lot of its impact. The first sentence would be

The stone is polished and bright like a dark brown eye that stares and glares at me.

2 Write out the second stanza as a sentence in normal English. You should see that writing the lines out like this causes a lot of the impact to be lost.

Deciding where to start new lines in your own poetry is a matter of choice. Generally speaking, you should start a new line wherever you feel a new idea begins. At any rate, your own lines of poetry shouldn't be much longer than those in *The Angry Stone.*

Start a new stanza (as you would a new paragraph) when a whole idea is completed.

3 What are the two separate stanzas of *The Angry Stone* about?

Making poems rhyme is difficult to do well and is only one part of poetry. There is no need to make poems rhyme until and unless you feel confident with this form of writing. If you enjoy rhyming, there is nothing to stop you practising the technique at points within the poem.

4 Which two words rhyme in *The Angry Stone?*

People write poetry for all sorts of different reasons. One of the main reasons is to express themselves in new ways about commonplace things, like stones. Writing in an interesting way about things we see all the time can give us a fresh view of the world.

5 *The Angry Stone* starts off with two adjectives that give a quick description.

 a Which two adjectives describe the stone in the first line?

 b What does the writer do to show that she is moving on from this quick description?

 c What is the stone compared to in the second line?

 d What does the writer do to show she is moving on from the first part of this comparison?

6 Poetry often makes use of verbs in interesting ways.

 a Which two verbs are used in the third line of the first stanza?

 b How are these verbs linked to the simile (the comparison) made earlier in the stanza?

 c What do these verbs make the writer feel about the stone?

When non-human things are made to seem human the effect is known as **personification**. The stone is made to seem human (it is *personified*) by the simile comparing it to an eye and then by the verbs that help to continue the comparison.

7 a Which two words continue the personification in the second stanza?

 b Which verb describes the way the writer picked up the stone from the beach?

 c What does this suggest about the way the stone was taken from the beach?

Revision booster

Write a short poem of your own about any commonplace object. It need be no longer than a couple of stanzas of three lines each. When you have thought of an object to describe, bring it to life with a comparison and verbs that create the effect of personification. Use what you have learned in this unit to guide your writing.

How did I do?

I know how to create impact with descriptive language.

47: Making comparisons

In this unit you will learn
▶ to make comparisons for clarity and effect

Get started

Comparing one thing with another thing (saying *this thing is like that thing*) often helps to make writing clearer and more effective. One of the easiest ways to make good comparisons is by using the words *like* and *as*.

Comparisons that use the words *like* and *as* are called **similes**.

The dog is *like* a vacuum cleaner.

The caves were *as* black *as* night.

In the first example the dog is being compared to a vacuum cleaner.

In the second example the darkness of the caves is compared to the blackness of night.

Both comparisons will work with either *like* or *as*, or you can use different words.

The dog cleans the floor *as* efficiently *as* a vacuum cleaner.

The dog *reminds me* of a vacuum cleaner.

Inside the caves it was *like* night.

Practice

1 Compare these ten things using either *like* or *as*. Use at least two examples of each.

a The acrobat and a cat

b Luke's shirt and a dishcloth

c The dragon's eye and a polished ruby

d The alien's fingernails and an eagle's talons

e The 4x4 and a battleship

As a writer you should notice now that your choice between *like* and *as* depends on how much detail you want to give your reader. For example, if you chose to write

The acrobat is *like* a cat

you are expecting your reader to understand the comparison without any extra help.

If you decided to write

The acrobat is *as* agile *as* a cat

then you are helping your reader to understand why you have made the comparison. You make it clear that it is the agility of the acrobat that reminds you of the agility of cats.

 Comparisons help to make writing clearer and more effective.

2 Create new similes by adding to these phrases. Choose whether to give the reader more help with the comparison (by using *as*) or less (by using *like*).

a The giant's footsteps

b Eva's eyes

c The shark's teeth

Comparisons using similes can help make descriptions clearer.

Ornithopods had strange faces.

Brachiosaurus' toe was 30 centimetres long.

Plateosaurus had unusual teeth.

This information can be rewritten like this

*Ornithopods had faces **like** horses.*

*Brachiosaurus' toe was **as long as** a man's forearm.*

*Plateosaurus had teeth shaped **like** long, thin pencils.*

3 Use similes to add detail to these statements.

a T Rex was six metres tall.

b Some dinosaurs could reach speeds of 110 kph.

Revision booster

As well as making things clearer, similes can also heighten effect. You can see this in some of the dinosaur statements in question 3. Your own simile about T Rex has probably made this creature seem more frightening than the original description of its height.

4 Describe the following, using similes to add effect.

a an octopus' tentacles

b an enormous dog

c a colourful parrot

How did I do?

I can make comparisons for clarity and effect. ☐

48: Writing description

Get started

Anyone who writes imaginatively has to balance description with action. In the following passage, the first sentence is descriptive and the second refers to an action.

The old man sat in the corner of the room. The telephone rang and the old man went to answer it.

The first sentence describes the old man. The second sentence relates to his actions when the telephone rings.

Practice

1 State whether each of the following sentences relates to a description or an action.

a *The little girl was dressed in red.*

b *The boy leapt into the pond.*

c *The bird was large and clumsy.*

d *All was still and the factory lay deserted.*

e *Everyone screamed and shouted as the ride began.*

In practice, of course, description and action are often presented in one and the same sentence.

The little girl with red hair leapt into the pond.

It is very common, however, for students to concentrate far too much on action when they write imaginatively. If the focus is too much on action, then this is the sort of text that can result.

> The old man sat in the corner of the room. The telephone rang and the old man went to answer it. He spoke for a while and then put the phone down. He opened the door and walked out. He went down the street as fast as he could. He stopped at the bus stop. A bus came and he got on. He went to the middle of town.

Imaginative writing is much more interesting if it contains more description than the text above. Good description is worth lots of marks in well-written fiction.

> The lonely old man sat in the corner of the room. His bleary eyes looked sadly out into the gloom. His face was a cobweb of wrinkles. Outside, the rain fell steadily. It ran down the window pane like tears down unhappy cheeks. In the distance, a telephone rang. The old man rose slowly, painfully from his chair.

The second passage about the old man is far more *descriptive*. The reader is given a much better sense of the feeling that surrounds the old man and his setting. The writer has created a much more interesting text using just a few simple techniques.

2 a The opening sentences of both passages are identical but for one word. Which one?

b What adjective is used in the second sentence to describe the old man's eyes?

c Which adverb describes the way the man's eyes are looking out?

d What noun describes where the man is looking?

e What impression do you get of the old man and his surroundings in the opening two sentences?

Recall that adverbs are used mainly to describe and give detail to verbs. The adverb you've identified in **2c** above describes (or modifies) the verb *looked*.

3 a What adverb is used to modify the verb *fell*?

b How is the rain made to seem more gloomy with this adverb?

Sometimes adverbs are used in pairs, to emphasise the intended effect.

The rain fell relentlessly, constantly.

4 Which adverbs in the text does the writer use for this descriptive technique?

Revision booster

Similes and metaphors are excellent ways of adding depth to a description. The writer of the second passage has used both. Remember that similes and metaphors are used to create comparisons between one thing and another. They create a picture (an *image*) in the mind of the reader.

5 What is the old man's face compared to?

A simile is a comparison introduced with the word *like* or *as*.

6 What two things in the passage are compared with a simile?

> ! Simple techniques used well can add great depth to descriptions. This unit has looked at the way adverbs, adjectives, similes and metaphors can be used carefully for this purpose.

How did I do?

I can consider descriptive techniques.   ✔ ☐

49: Description

In this unit you will learn
▶ to develop descriptive technique

Get started

Read the following text. It was written by a Year 9 pupil called Alex.

The boy walked into the room. There was a picture on the wall. It was a picture of a man. The man's eyes seemed to follow the boy as he walked through the door. A woman came down the stairs towards the boy.

Practice

1 a What sort of text do you think Alex is writing?

b Explain your reason for thinking this.

Alex uses one extremely good descriptive technique. This technique is to follow a noun phrase with either the verb *seem* or *appear*. It creates the *impression* that something is going on which the writer is not sure of or does not fully understand. Here are some examples of this useful technique.

*The beast **appeared** to be sleeping.*

*The television **seemed** to have been turned on.*

*The statue **appeared** to move.*

This form of words suggests to the reader that the person telling the story is not sure of what they say. You can add a phrase like *but I wasn't sure* to any of these sentences in order to appreciate this point fully—. Uncertainty creates a sense that the storyteller is telling the truth and it creates mystery and suspense. If you remove *appeared* or *seemed* from any of these sentences you will understand this point more clearly. For example

The television had been turned on.

2 Write out the other two sentences in the list. Remove the word *appeared* and reorganise the rest of the words so that the new sentence makes sense. Notice how the uncertainty and suspense disappears.

3 a In which sentence does Alex use this technique to create uncertainty and suspense?

b Remove the word *seemed* from Alex's sentence and reorganise the rest of the words so that the new sentence makes good sense. Notice how the suspense is affected.

The adverb at the end of the second sentence modifies a verb that is also used to create a rather mournful mood.

4 What is the verb that is modified at the end of the second sentence?

One of the most effective techniques of description open to a writer is the use of contrast. This is not surprising, really, when you think of some examples from everyday life. Stars, for instance, are in the sky the whole time. It is only when it's dark that you see them because they contrast with the blackness of the night.

In the passage about the waiting room, the writer wants to create a mood that is in tune with his own gloomy feelings as he waits for the dentist. He highlights and emphasises this mood with the contrasts introduced at the end.

5 a Which adjectives are used in the final sentence to emphasise the faces and the smiles on the magazines' covers?

b Remember the continuous participle. It is created by adding *ing* to the infinitive form of a verb. Which participle suggests the way the faces and smiles shine out from the magazines?

c How does the real world of the waiting room contrast with the make-believe world of the magazines?

 Use foregrounded prepositional phrases to create variety in your own writing.

It is important to vary word order in sentences. If sentences are not varied, then writing, even in short extracts like this, can become repetitive. One of the easiest and most effective ways of varying sentence structure is by foregrounding prepositional phrases. In the third sentence the writer of the extract foregrounds the phrase *On a table.*

On a table in the middle of the room were some crumpled, glossy magazines.

This could have been written

Some crumpled, glossy magazines were on a table in the middle of the room.

The writer also foregrounds a prepositional phrase at the start of the second sentence.

6 Rearrange the sentence using the example above as your guide.

Now reread the whole passage with the reorganised sentences. Notice how repetitive it seems.

How did I do?

I know how to consider the creation of mood. ☐

52: Creating mood (2)

In this unit you will learn
- ▶ to study the creation of mood

Get started

Read this extract from a short story called *The Empty Room.* Edmund, a boy of thirteen, is about to enter the house he was taken from as a baby.

> I stood on the doorstep, collecting my thoughts. As I stood, silently, fearfully, I reflected that the night seemed suddenly to have grown much colder. This cursed house seemed to be alive, its icy breath chilling the air around it. I resolved, finally, to go in. I reached for the knocker, and as I did so, the door swung silently open.

Practice

1 On the evidence of this paragraph alone, what kind of story do you think this is?

2 a How do Edmund's actions in the first sentence create a tense atmosphere?

  b Which two adverbs, next to each other in the second sentence, add to the tension?

The house is described as a living thing. It is personified.

3 a What does the house seem to be doing?

  b What effect does this have on our view of the house?

4 Which word, repeated twice in the passage, appeals to the reader's sense of sound?

5 Explain why the last sentence increases the sense of tension.

Adverbs are a group of describing words that often end in the letters *ly*. They can be very important in creating mood and atmosphere.

In the passage from *The Empty Room* there are five adverbs ending in *ly.*

Adverbs can create different types of mood, for example, a happy mood, an excited mood, a sad mood.

6 a Locate these five adverbs and write them down in the order they appear.

  b Read the passage again but leave the adverbs out. Does the writing still make sense?

  c What effect has been created by leaving out the adverbs?

Edmund now enters the house and walks down the passageway.

> *I walked hesitantly into the dusky interior of the house. Beneath my feet was a carpet, a red carpet, that I seemed to remember from long ago. The colour was near, at least in this gloomy light, to that of dried blood. With cautious steps, I advanced further into the looming shadows. There was still no sound, no movement, no sign of life.*
>
> *And then, far, far away upstairs, the faint sound of a crying baby.*

There are three references in this passage to the sense of sight. The first of these is *dusky interior* in the first sentence.

7 a Write down the two other phrases that appeal to the reader's sense of sight.

b Taken together, what impression do these three phrases create of the inside of the house?

8 a Write down two phrases that describe the way Edmund walks into the house.

b Why does Edmund move in this way?

A **simile** is a comparison between two things.

9 a In this passage, a simile is used to compare the colour of the carpet to the colour of what?

b What activities might the simile suggest to the reader?

These questions all refer to the last sentence of the passage.

10 a How are the contents of this sentence different from the rest of the passage?

b How is the sentence placed so as to emphasise its difference?

c What word is repeated to emphasise the distance of the crying baby from Edmund?

d How else is the baby's distance from Edmund made clear?

e How does the baby's presence increase the sense of tension?

Revision booster

Write your own introduction to a story about entering a gloomy place. Make use of
- adverbs
- personification
- references to sound and sight
- unusual similes

How did I do?

I can study the creation of mood.

✔
☐

53: Focus in writing

In this unit you will learn
- ▶ to describe short episodes in detail

Get started

A problem writers often have when they are describing an experience is deciding exactly what part of that experience to focus on. To get round this difficulty, they often decide to write about everything they can think of or remember.

This is a description of a race.

> I came out of the changing room and walked down to the track. All the other runners were there. We tied our laces ready to begin. The starter came down with the pistol. The pistol was fired and the race began. I ran as fast as I could but could only come fourth. After the race I was exhausted.

This account is a summary of the race, from start to finish.

Practice

1 Using between five and ten short sentences, write your own account of a complete sporting event. Use the description of the race as your guide. You could write about

- ● a team game you have played in

- ● an athletics event

- ● an individual sporting performance

The really important thing is to cover everything. For example, if you were writing about a game of rugby or netball, you would include details of the game from the kick-off to the final whistle. You could also include things such as getting changed before the game and coming off at the end. Do not use more than ten sentences.

A good way to improve the focus of your writing is to ask *yourself* these kinds of questions. Do it before you start and continue to do it as you write.

Accounts such as these are called **summaries**. They are complete but they do leave lots of questions unanswered. Any interested reader would want to know things like

- ● What were the other runners like?

- ● Were you confident before the race began?

- ● How did you feel as the race was going on?

2 Write down three more questions it would be interesting to ask the writer of the race description.

The first part of the race description is *I came out of the changing room.* Consider the sort of questions that could be asked about this first half-sentence.

- What did the changing room door look like?

- How did the doorknob feel?

- What was the effect of light and shade?

- Was there a difference in temperature between inside and out?

Look back at your own description of a sporting event. Choose one area to focus on. It could be as little as half a sentence.

3 Make a short list of interesting questions that could be asked about this part of your account. Use the questions above as a guide.

Questions can be answered before and as you are writing.

As I walked towards the changing room door, I noticed that the paint was cracked and peeling. I opened the door and felt the handle slip a little out of my grasp. My hands were wet with perspiration. As the door swung open, I was dazzled by the bright light after the gloom inside. I gasped as the cold air hit my throat.

4 The first question in the list above is answered by the first sentence of this new description. Look again at the other three questions. Which sentences are used to answer each of them?

5 Go back to your own sporting description from question 1. You have already chosen a part of it to develop. Write a new description that is focused on the part you chose. As you write, use

- the questions you asked yourself in question 2

- the focused description of the changing room as a guide

Revision booster

Choose another small area to focus on from your own description of a sporting event. Ask yourself at least four questions that could be answered to add interest to this area of focus. Rewrite the description so that the answers are included in a detailed account.

How did I do?

I can describe short episodes in detail.   ☐

54: Conveying feelings

Get started

Erin Maskey lives in a small village or 'kampung' in Malaysia and writes regularly about her experiences there. Here she describes her village and the fear of snakes that nearly stopped her from going there at all.

> When most of my friends arrive in kampung Kerinchi they think it's terrible. They see it as completely disorganised and chaotic. In my opinion it's a paradise on Earth. I love the gentleness of the people here and I adore the relaxed and peaceful attitude they have towards life. The chaos described by my friends is, in my view, just the constant clatter, rattle and hum of a busy village. When you see the vibrant, rainbow colours of the women's clothes and taste the exquisite local dishes, so full of flavour, you realise you're somewhere very special.
>
> The thing that almost prevented me from coming to live in a kampung was the abundance of snakes. I was utterly terrified of them. To my way of thinking they were the creatures of which I was by far the most frightened. I'd felt this way since childhood in England when I opened a picnic lunchbox and a grass snake had slithered out onto my lap. As an adult, I knew that my feelings about these animals were ridiculous, and I felt foolish, but I couldn't help it. I even had a recurring nightmare of waking up undigested in a snake's stomach. That's how bad it was.

Practice

1 a List three adjectives that describe the view Erin's friends have of kampung Kerinchi.

   b What phrase does Erin use in the third sentence to describe her view of the kampung?

   c Write down two of the reasons Erin gives for feeling the way she does.

2 a Write down two adjectives that describe Erin's feelings about snakes.

   b What had happened in her childhood to make her feel this way?

   c How did this attitude towards snakes make her feel as an adult?

We often quote from texts to give greater impact to what we want to say.

Compare these two sentences.

Erin says she dreams of snakes.

Erin says she dreams of 'waking up undigested in a snake's stomach'.

The second sentence is based on the original but includes a good quotation from the passage.

3 Base new sentences with good quotations from the passage on the originals below. Use the example comparison as a guide and don't forget to include quotation marks. Write each sentence out in full and begin with, *Erin says she likes ...*

a Erin says she likes the villagers.

b Erin says she likes the noises of the village.

c Erin says she likes the clothes the women wear.

d Erin says she likes the food.

> Erin now describes an encounter in the kampung with a 5-metre-long Burmese Python.
>
> I was pulling up some weeds one morning in the garden around my hut when I sensed what at first felt like a hand grasp my ankle. When I looked down I saw this mass of rippling dark flesh wrapping itself around my leg like some evil climbing plant. I had trodden on a python and it was starting to constrict. I opened my mouth to scream but no sound came out. My upper body, which was free, was as immobile as my legs, which were by now enveloped by the python. I stood as still as a statue, literally paralysed. And then the python unwound itself and slowly made its way off. It didn't want to harm me. My own feeling about this strange episode is that it understood my 'aggression' was an accident. In a second, my fear of snakes disappeared and it has never come back.

4

a What is the snake compared to in the opening sentences to emphasise Erin's fear?

b How does Erin's terror affect her physical ability to function?

c Why do you think Erin chooses to put the word 'aggression' between inverted commas?

d What benefit comes from the incident with the python?

Revision booster

You can often spot where writers introduce their own ideas because they use phrases like

In my opinion

In my view

To my way of thinking

My own feeling about this

5 Find examples in both texts where Erin introduces her ideas like this.

6 Read a travel article in a Sunday newspaper. Highlight places in the text where the writer's own ideas and opinions are expressed.

How did I do?

I can investigate how writers convey feelings. ✔ ☐

55: Character in fiction (1)

In this unit you will learn
- ▶ to interpret character in literary texts

Get started

Around the ages of five or six years old, children often read simple texts like this.

> Benjamin Bear was very kind. In fact, he was the kindest, most gentle bear in the whole of Cuddleland.

There are two important things for you to notice about this short text. First of all, it is about a character (in this case, a bear, but it could be a person, an imaginary being or a mythological beast). Stories written for the youngest children and for adults are centred on character because that is what readers find most interesting.

The second thing you must notice about the text is that it *tells* its young readers what to think. Nothing has been suggested about Benjamin Bear. Nothing has to be inferred or interpreted by the reader. The young reader understands what Benjamin Bear is about because he or she is *told what to think* about him.

Practice

1 Find the two or three adjectives in the extract above that tell the reader what to think about Benjamin's character.

Texts for older readers do not present character in the *Benjamin Bear* sort of way.

> Sammy Sneak crept silently to the side of the shed. His greasy black hair was piled up into an enormous quiff. His purple and black trouser suit clung to him tightly. Catching sight of himself in the shed's dusty window, he allowed himself a grin. He was, as usual, delighted with his appearance. Still on tiptoe, he pressed his ear to the side of the shed and listened.

This is a very different text, and not just because it is longer. This text forces the reader to think, to make inferences about a character. It makes the reader *interpret* what Sammy Sneak is like.

2
a In no more than a sentence, express your opinion of Sammy Sneak's appearance.

b What does Sammy think of the way he looks?

c What do Sammy's feelings about his appearance suggest about his character?

d What is Sammy actually doing in this extract (apart from looking at himself) that gives the reader a rather poor impression of him?

Interesting fiction can create characters that are 'larger than life'.

Think about people you know well. You cannot know everything about them. You have to make inferences about their characters (are they kind, are they mean, can I trust them?) based on what they are like or what they do. A good story presents readers with characters that they must interpret in just the same way.

Look back at the *Benjamin Bear* text. Although it tells us what to think about Benjamin Bear, the reader is allowed to make a basic inference about the kind of place he lives in.

3 a What inference can the reader make about the type of place Benjamin Bear lives in?

b Look again at the two proper nouns (next to one another) in the second extract. What can the reader confidently infer from the second proper noun?

Now read the second part of the *Sammy Sneak* text.

> Inside the shed, the five children were discussing their plans to build a new tree house.
>
> 'It'll be fantastic,' said Jennifer. 'We're going to have so much fun.'
>
> 'Yeah,' replied Data. 'We'll be able to take picnics, play games, do all sorts of cool stuff. I can even take my laptop up there.'
>
> 'I can't wait to get started,' said Lycos. 'Let's draw up the plans now.'
>
> Outside the shed, Sammy Sneak's lips curled into the shadow of a smile. His plans for the tree house were somewhat different.

Notice that nowhere in the text is the reader told what to think about anyone or anything. All the reader's conclusions must be inferred.

4 a Sum up in a single sentence the mood of the children inside the shed.

b Which of the children is into technology and why do you infer this?

c What, roughly, do you think that Sammy's plans will involve?

How did I do?

I can interpret character in literary texts.   ☐

56: Character in fiction (2)

In this unit you will learn
▶ to create character in fiction

Get started

Writers have a few basic means of describing the characters they choose to place in their texts.

● They can refer to them neutrally with pronouns and nouns.

He lived next door.

Mrs Thorpe was 29 years old.

● Writers can develop character, if they wish, by using adjectives.

Mrs Thorpe was happy.

● Writers can also *reveal* character by describing what people actually *do*.

He slipped quietly through the door.

Practice

1 a What verb and adverb combination is used to describe the character's actions in the last sentence above?

b What *might* these actions reveal about the personality and situation of this character?

In your own writing, you should use all of these different ways of referring to character. It is the last way, though, that most students need to practise. Character that is *revealed* is much more interesting and much closer to real life. Read the following passage.

> The sick man lay still on the bed. Jonah looked tenderly down at him. Every few moments, he moistened the flannel and bathed his brother's forehead. When he was sure his patient slept, he slipped quietly through the door.

2 Look at the second sentence of the passage.

a What adverb is used to describe the way Jonah acts?

b What is Jonah actually doing for his brother?

c Why does he slip quietly through the door?

3 Compare your last answer with the one you gave to the similar question in 1b. It is almost certainly different, perhaps very different. What has caused your answer to change?

If you were asked to sum up Jonah's character in sentences containing adjectives, you would probably arrive at this sort of thing.

Jonah was kind.

Jonah was tender.

There is a place for sentences like these. It is preferable on most occasions, however, to give readers the evidence and let them come to their own conclusions. Your own fictional style will improve (as will your marks) if you use the approach used above.

Read the following vivid character description.

> I sat trembling as Humbert's balloon face leered up at me. At first, his mouth was closed in a thin line and his eyes were narrowed. He looked at me silently and with total contempt. His nose seemed to wrinkle up in disgust at my very presence. Suddenly his mouth opened to reveal uneven yellow teeth and an enormous pink tongue. He shouted abuse, and as he did so, covered me in flecks of spit.

Characterisation is the art of creating fictional character. The *narrator* is hardly characterised here at all except by the use of a single adjective.

4 Which adjective is used to characterise the narrator and show his fear?

Humbert is characterised in detail. This is mainly done through his facial features.

5 How are the following of Humbert's features described?

  a face

  b eyes

  c teeth

6 Which other of Humbert's facial features are also described?

7 What unpleasant *physical* thing happens to the narrator at the end of the extract?

Revision booster

Based on the evidence *revealed* in the passage above, it is unlikely that you would write the following adjectival statement about Humbert.

Humbert was a kind and attractive man.

8 What would you write?

Note how much less effective such statements are than those that *reveal* character through a description of behaviour.

How did I do?

I can create character in fiction.

✔

! Character that is revealed is much more interesting for readers. This is because readers wish to discover things for themselves, much as they do in real life.

57: Creating character

In this unit you will learn
 ▶ to create engaging fictional characters

Get started

Read the following description.

> Maxi walked into the room. He was short but strong looking. He had blue eyes. His mouth was closed. When he opened his mouth, a chipped front tooth could be seen. He gave his orders, then left.

Practice

1 This description concentrates on Maxi's appearance. List four permanent features of Maxi's appearance.

2 In no more than six short sentences, write your own description of a person. Start off with the person walking into a room, as in the passage about Maxi. Concentrate only on the appearance of the person you are describing.

Adjectives are excellent tools for helping writers build up descriptions of personality.

Writers can add to the description of a person's appearance by including detail about personality. This can easily be done by using **adjectives** in new sentences.

*Maxi was a **cruel** and **wicked** person.*

*Maxi was a **sad** and **jealous** man.*

3 Add two new sentences with adjectives to your own description.

Adjectives can also give greater detail to sentences already in a text.

*He had **cruel** blue eyes.*

*He had **piercing** blue eyes.*

4 Add two adjectives to sentences that are already in your description. You should choose adjectives that help you to develop the kind of character you want to create.

Adverbs (words used to describe verbs) can help with your description in the same way as adjectives.

*Maxi walked **quietly** into the room.*

*His piercing blue eyes darted about **suspiciously**.*

5 Look back at your own description and add detail with one or two adverbs.

Using **comparisons** is another way of developing a description.

*He was short, but looked **as strong and square as a brick**.*

*His chipped front tooth **looked like a broken tombstone**.*

6 Use comparisons to add colour and detail to your own description.

This unit has looked at some of the ways in which writers can develop descriptions of character. These have included

● describing appearance

● using adjectives

● using adverbs

● making comparisons

Using these techniques, the original description of Maxi walking into a room can be turned into something much more dramatic and interesting.

> Maxi walked quietly into the shabby room. He was a short man but he looked as strong and square as a brick. His piercing blue eyes darted about suspiciously from person to person. His mouth stayed briefly closed. When he opened it to speak, his chipped front tooth stood out like a broken tombstone. He gave his orders briefly, then left. Maxi was indeed a cruel and wicked man.

7 Compare this description with the one of Maxi at the beginning of the unit. What do we now know about Maxi that we didn't know before?

Revision booster

Return to your own description of a character walking into a room. Use the notes you have made in this unit to make the description more entertaining and dramatic. Develop your description in exactly the same way as the account of Maxi was built up. You do not, of course, need to describe a dark and wicked character.

How did I do?

I can create engaging fictional characters. ☐

58: Assessing character

In this unit you will learn
▶ to assess and interpret character

Get started

Abigail Loasby is an endurance cyclist who takes on challenges designed to push her mind and body to their limits. One of her recent challenges was to cycle from Scotland to Cornwall in five days. Here, she describes a part of her journey.

750 miles in five days was going to be hard. I'm not a mathematician, but even I could work out that an average of 150 miles a day would test the toughest legs. Not that I was too worried about this particular part of my anatomy. The worst part of long-distance cycling is what happens to your backside. Saddle sore, as cyclists know it, is agonising. It creeps up on you and the pain becomes so blinding you can't sit down. It's the only thing that's ever come close to beating me. Not that car drivers don't try their best to make a mess of things too. Their thoughtless behaviour has often left me upended in country ditches or sprawled on a pavement, but they haven't stopped me yet ...

In fact, in the middle of this ride, I did come off, but there were no cars around and it was entirely my own fault. I braked too sharply for some reason, flew over the handlebars and crashed into a tree. My mouth filled up with blood and, as I spat, one of my front teeth flew out. I later found out that the impact had broken my nose, but I didn't worry about that at the time. Once I'd shaken off my dizziness, I got back on the bike and cycled off the pain. If you're going to be an endurance athlete you need to be strong, you need to be obstinate and you need to treat pain with contempt.

Practice

1. These questions focus on the first paragraph.

   a What numbers does Abigail mention in her first sentence?

   b Why do you think Abigail chooses to start her account like this?

   c What does Abigail say is the most painful part of long-distance cycling?

   d Which two words are chosen to emphasise this pain?

   e What one word sums up Abigail's view of drivers' behaviour?

2. The following questions focus on the second paragraph.

   a Read the end of the first sentence. What does it suggest to us about Abigail?

   b What injuries does Abigail pick up when she flies over her handlebars?

c What does Abigail's response to her accident indicate about her character?

d Which part of the extract emphasises the three things needed to be an endurance athlete?

! Look at what characters do. Their actions tell us a lot about their personalities.

In this section, Abigail writes about her love of cycling and the change in her attitude towards endurance events.

> When I was a teenager, I used to think endurance challenges were for freaks. But then, one birthday, I was given a new bike and my feelings changed completely. I was out on the bike every day and every day I wanted to push myself harder. I came to see my bike as a friend, a partner in my struggle to overcome any obstacles. Now as an adult, I think endurance events present enormous challenges and give tremendous benefits to all involved.

3 a How have Abigail's feelings changed towards endurance events?

b What single gift sparked this change in her attitude?

c How does Abigail emphasise the strong feelings she had for her bike?

Here, Abigail describes the way a fellow cyclist fails to complete the challenge.

> On the evening of the third day, I could see that Evelyn was dropping further and further behind. I could feel myself becoming impatient. It got to the stage where I stopped, waited for her and then let her have it with both barrels. I told her to finish now if she couldn't make it and stop dragging me back. I told her I was sick of people who didn't prepare themselves properly. I guess I was a bit hard and Evelyn dissolved into tears. As I cycled off I felt a bit sorry – but I knew I'd done the right thing.

4 What does this episode suggest about Abigail's personality? Write about

● her feelings when Evelyn starts to slow down

● the way Abigail talks to Evelyn and what this suggests about her

● her feelings afterwards

● what Abigail's actions show us about her personality.

Revision booster

Find other accounts of endurance adventures. There are lots of them. Look particularly at the challenges faced by the participants and the way they are overcome. What are the similarities between the stories you read and the extracts from Abigail Loasby's account?

How did I do?

I can assess and interpret character. ✔ ☐

59: Speech in literature

In this unit you will learn
> • to analyse speech in a classic text

Get started

Read this passage from *The Yellow Wallpaper,* an extraordinary short story by a writer called Charlotte Perkins Gilman. It is an account of a woman, told in her own words, who is slowly going mad. One of the symptoms of her madness is that she believes there is a female prisoner behind the patterned wallpaper in her bedroom. In this scene, she wakes up in the middle of the night with her husband, John, beside her.

> John was asleep and I hated to waken him, so I kept still and watched the moonlight on that undulating wallpaper till I felt creepy.
>
> The faint figure behind seemed to shake the pattern, just as if she wanted to get out.
>
> I got up softly and went to feel and see if the paper did move, and when I came back John was awake.
>
> "What is it little girl?" he said. "Don't go walking about like that – you'll get cold."
>
> I thought it was a good time to talk, so I told him that I was not gaining here, and that I wished he would take me away.
>
> "Why darling!" said he. "Our lease will be up in three weeks, and I can't see how to leave before."

Practice

1 The narrator (the woman slowly going mad) is childlike.

    a Which word at the end of the first sentence seems a little childlike?

    b Which (two-word) noun phrase suggests that her husband views her as a child?

Structures can be childlike, as well as vocabulary. Look at the following example.

"Can I have my present yet?" I asked Daddy.

"Not yet," replied he.

The word *Daddy* is nowadays seen as childlike. The word order *replied he* is also childlike.

2 a Write out these two words (*replied he*) in their usual order.

    b Where might you find a structure like this?

    c Write out the example of this structure used in the passage above.

3 What verb does the narrator use to describe the actions of the figure behind the wallpaper pattern?

Read the whole of *The Yellow Wallpaper*. It is a breathtaking and terrifying account of a woman's descent into madness.

Remember *imagery,* the art of creating a picture in a reader's mind.

4 What picture is suggested by the verb you identified in question 3?

5 The narrator has a childlike fascination in what she thinks she sees. What does she do that proves she is *certain* she saw *something* in the wallpaper?

The conversation between the narrator and her husband continues like this.

> "I don't weigh a bit more," said I, "nor as much; and my appetite may be better in the evening when you are here but it is worse in the morning when you are away!"
>
> "Bless her little heart," said he with a big hug. "She shall be as sick as she pleases ... Really, dear, you are better!"
>
> "Better in body, perhaps –" I began ...

Younger (and sometimes older) children often try hard to avoid upsetting or disturbing their parents. The narrator is like this with her husband.

6 What does she try to avoid doing to John at the start of the first passage?

7 In this passage, the reader learns that she does something only when John is there. What does the narrator do properly only when her husband is with her?

She avoids finishing her sentence at the end of this passage to avoid upsetting John.

8 What was she about to say that would have upset her husband?

Revision booster

John uses the determiner *her* and the pronoun *she.*

9
a What is so odd about using these two words *in this situation*?
b In which situations might it be normal for people to use language like this?

How did I do?

I can analyse speech in a classic text.   ☐ ✔

60: Formal and informal (1)

In this unit you will learn

▶ to adapt style to audience and purpose

Get started

There is no right or wrong writing style. There are simply many styles to choose from. Some of them will be right on one occasion. Others will be right on different occasions. Learning when to use the range of available styles is an important part of becoming a better writer.

Style refers to the way you choose to write. Read this extract from an e-mail circular.

> Hi guys! Sorry not to have been in touch for so long. I'm in Australia now (whooeee!) and here's my new address.

The writer uses a **relaxed style**, which is signalled at the opening of her e-mail.

Practice

1 a Which two words does the writer use at the start of her e-mail to create informality?

b What punctuation mark does she use twice to suggest energy and fun?

c Which onomatopoeic (sound related) word does she use to show her excitement?

Remember that sometimes an adjective can follow a verb to describe a subject. For example

I am happy.

Donna is pleased.

In very informal writing, the initial subject and the verb can be missed out as follows.

Happy you could make it!

Pleased that you could come!

2 Write out the sentence from the e-mail in which the writer uses this informal technique.

Contraction of words is also a sign of informality. This happens when writers join two words with an apostrophe and 'lose' letters to imitate speech. For example

will not   becomes   *won't*

he will   becomes   *he'll*

3   a Write down the two contracted forms in the e-mail.

b What would be the formal way of writing out these words?

The writer of the e-mail used exactly the right sort of style for her purpose. She wanted to communicate with her friends in a way that was clear, purposeful, fun and relaxed. And this is exactly what she did. As it happens, however, the same author writes instructions for flat pack manuals. The following extract is from one of her leaflets.

> Press down firmly with both hands. Next, push the rockers into place. The chair is now ready to use.

These are instructions. The writing contains features of an **instructional style** in just the same way as the informal e-mail had *its* own special features.

A feature of instructions is that they need to be laid out clearly according to what happens when. This means that adverbs describing *when* things happen are common. These include words like

soon   firstly   now   next   then   finally

4   Which two adverbs from this list can you find in the flat pack text?

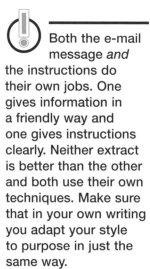 Both the e-mail message *and* the instructions do their own jobs. One gives information in a friendly way and one gives instructions clearly. Neither extract is better than the other and both use their own techniques. Make sure that in your own writing you adapt your style to purpose in just the same way.

Most sentences have a subject and a verb. You have already seen how this rule can be broken in certain types of informal writing. However, writing to instruct also breaks this rule. Subjects are often missed out in order to give a direct instruction. For example

grind the pepper   not   *you* grind the pepper

whisk the eggs   not   *you* whisk the eggs

screw down the lid   not   *you* screw down the lid

5   Write down the two sentences in the extract that use this technique.

How did I do?

I can adapt style to audience and purpose.   ☐

61: Formal and informal (2)

In this unit you will learn
- to adapt texts for informality

Get started

Read this party invitation.

Dear (fill in guest's name)

I am having a party on Saturday, 13th May to which you are invited. It will be at the local pool with food and drink provided. Before the refreshment, there will be games and other activities both in the pool and the garden outside. I expect a quick reply to this invitation so that I do not order more guest places for the party than is necessary.

Yours sincerely,

Chloe-Louise

Practice

1
a Who is Chloe-Louise's audience for this letter?

b What is Chloe-Louise's purpose in writing this letter?

c Explain in a sentence how Chloe-Louise has misunderstood her audience and purpose.

Chloe-Louise's good friend Shauna saw the invitations before they were sent out. The two of them rewrote the invitations together. This is what they came up with.

Hi (fill in guest's name)!

I'm having a party on Saturday, 13th May and I'd really love you to come. It's going to be at the SeaSpray Centre so there's absolutely loads to do when you get there. Wave machines, the 60-metre slide, the Devil's Rapids – choose your thrill! When we've had as much fun as we can handle it'll be time for the Old Ranch barbecue in the SeaSpray gardens. If you've not had one of their Smoky Joe burgers, you haven't lived.

Can you make it? Tell me as soon as you can. I look forward to seeing you there!

Chloe-Louise

2
a Why have the girls changed the way the guest is greeted at the start of the letter?

b Why do you think they mention the SeaSpray Centre by name in the second letter?

c How does Chloe-Louise seem to feel towards her friends at the end of the first letter?

d How do her feelings seem to have changed by the end of the second letter?

 Imperatives, direct questions and exclamation marks are features of informal writing.

Sentences (or short phrases) that begin with a verb and give an instruction are called **imperatives**. The phrase *Choose your thrill* is an example. Imperatives are often used in this kind of letter because they are very direct.

3 Write down the imperative sentence used in the last paragraph of the second letter.

Questions are also used in this sort of letter to show a friendly directness.

4 Write down the direct, friendly question that is asked in the second letter.

Exclamation marks are another important feature of this sort of writing. They indicate that things are exciting and fun.

5 Write down an example of a fun-sounding sentence that ends with an exclamation mark.

> Chloe-Louise's second letter also improves on her first because it contains more interesting information.
>
> **6** From the second invitation, write down
>
> a three new items of information about the swimming pool
>
> b two items of information about the food

Revision booster

Write a party invitation of your own. Use an informal style and include examples of

● imperative sentences
● direct questions to your readers
● exclamation marks to finish fun-sounding sentences
● sentences with lots of detail about the events at the party

Use Chloe-Louise's second letter as a guide.

How did I do?

I can adapt texts for informality.   ✔ ☐

62: Instructions and advice

In this unit you will learn
> to present effective advice

Get started

Read the following piece of somewhat rude advice.

Sit down, shut up and listen.

Advice given very directly like this is close to being instruction.

Remember from Unit 15 that sentences within sentences are called clauses. There are three clauses within the short sentence above. They are

sit down   shut up   listen

Each of these three clauses begins with a verb, *sit*, *shut* or *listen*. Clauses, or sentences, that begin with a verb like this are called **imperative**. Imperatives are very common in writing that advises or instructs. Look at the following examples of this.

Overtake when you can see ahead.

Spend your money wisely.

Take care crossing the road.

There are three pieces of advice, all beginning with verbs. The verbs are *overtake*, *spend* and *take*. All these sentences are imperative.

Practice

1 Write three imperative sentences of your own that begin with the following verbs.

Drive   Stay   Put

There are, of course, imperative sentences that are negative. They advise or instruct someone *not* to do something. The following negative sentence starts with the words *do not* (shortened to *don't*).

Don't drive drunk.

2 Give three pieces of negative advice beginning with the following combinations.

Don't take

Don't waste

Don't go

Here is some advice for people who have burnt their hand on the cooker.

> Turn the cooker off immediately. If you are in pain, you could forget that it's on. Run the cold tap and fill a bowl with water. Plunge your hand into the water and leave it there until the pain subsides. You might find this happens quite soon. If the pain continues, you may want to see a doctor at the first opportunity. Do not put off doing this.

Imperatives are an excellent way of giving advice and instructions in very few words. If they are overused, though, a text will become repetitive.

3 a You should be able to find three imperative sentences in this text. Write down the opening verb of each one of them.

   b Write down the one negative imperative sentence.

Notice that advice and instructions are given *to* someone. There is no point providing advice if it's not clear who the advice is for.

4 What pronoun used four times in the text above indicates that the writer is speaking directly to an imagined reader?

Imperative sentences are very direct and if writers are too direct they will sometimes be thought rude. The first text in this unit is both imperative and rude. One way around rudeness (or nagging a reader with advice – *do this, do that*) is to use **modal verbs**. Modal verbs are verbs that tag along with normal verbs. They suggest rather than direct and they do the same thing as an imperative but much more politely. Here are some examples.

*You **might** want to write that letter now.*

*You **could** think about coming with me.*

*You **may** consider taking a chance.*

The first sentence uses the modal verb *might* in combination with the verb *want* to give some extremely polite advice. Expressed as an imperative the sentence would be

Write that letter now.

5 Write out the second and third sentences as imperatives.

6 The extract about the burnt hand uses modal verbs three times for politeness. Write out the modal verbs and the main verbs they combine with.

How did I do?

I can present effective advice. ✔ ☐

63: Informative style

In this unit you will learn
- ▶ to consider informative style

Get started

Read the following information regarding the famous ship *RMS Titanic.*

Completed in 1912, *RMS Titanic* was the world's most celebrated passenger ship. She was a vast and impressive colossus, the largest and most sumptuous liner in the world. This great ship was nearly 300 metres in length and each propeller was as large as a tennis court. In all, *Titanic* could hold over 3500 passengers, some of them in luxury previously unheard of. There were swimming pools, saunas and squash courts. Thought to be unsinkable, *Titanic* was equipped with magnetic chambers that were designed to close should they fill with water.

Practice

1 Where might you expect to find this kind of text?

Remember that **coherence** is an important part of texts. Coherence is a word that refers to the way a body of writing holds together. One way of developing coherence is by establishing clear noun chains (or reference chains) for the key noun phrases in the text. Look at the following example.

The snake slid through the undergrowth. This superb beast could be only dimly seen. Within seconds, she had disappeared.

! Vary your own noun references when you write to inform or describe. It will develop cohesion and interest in your text.

The key noun phrase in this passage is *the snake.* A chain is established throughout the short text that maintains the focus on the snake. It is formed like this.

the snake then *this superb beast* and finally *she*

Writers can create interest as well as coherence by varying the way they refer to their important noun phrases. When you are sure you can see the way the reference chain works in the snake passage, look at the extract on *Titanic.*

2 Make a reference chain for the key subject of this passage. The first two links in your chain are as follows.

RMS Titanic *the world's most celebrated passenger ship*

Look at the reference chain you have made. Notice just *how many* different ways the writer has found of referring to the same thing.

3 What impression has the writer conveyed of *Titanic* in the reference chain?

The writer makes various claims about *Titanic*'s size and luxury.

4   a Which two statistics are used to support the claim about *Titanic*'s size?

      b Write down the three facts provided to demonstrate *Titanic's* luxury.

Similes are often used in informative and descriptive writing. They are very useful in demonstrating sizes and volumes that are difficult to imagine. For example

A diplodocus was as long as a terrace of houses.

A cheetah can run as fast as a car.

The meteor was the size of Ireland.

Something which is unfamiliar to a reader is compared to something that may be more familiar. This enables the reader to visualise the thing being described. It therefore improves understanding.

5   What is the simile used for this purpose by the writer of the passage?

Remember that the present perfect tense is formed with *have* plus the perfect participle of the verb.

have completed

have begun

The combination can only work with the participle *begun*.

The perfect participle can then often be used at the beginning of sentences to form an interesting variation on normal structure. It is a variation that is often found in informative texts.

Begun *in 1909,* RMS Titanic *took three years to build.*

Two sentences in the *RMS Titanic* text begin with the perfect participle.

6   Write down the different participles that begin each of these sentences.

How did I do?

I can consider informative style.   ✔ ☐

64: Writing complaints

Get started

Adversarial texts are produced when a writer blames someone for something. The most common types of adversarial texts are letters of complaint. Here is an extract from such a letter received recently by a hotel owner in Wales.

> You claim that your hotel preserves 'the highest standards of quality and service'. I suggest that it did not do this on my family's visit last weekend.
>
> Your tiny car park was full when we arrived so we were forced to park half a mile away on a public road. After hauling our suitcases to the hotel, we were left standing at check-in for more than five minutes before a receptionist finally appeared. On top of this, our room was without soap or towels, a fact my daughter only discovered once she was in the shower.

Bold statements can be effective methods of drawing definite lines between two sides of a debate or argument. Verbs useful for this purpose are those such as

believe   suggest   claim   insist   protest   argue   feel   maintain

For example

*You **maintain** there is life on Pluto. I **believe** you are wrong.*

Practice

1 a Which two-word clause does the writer use at the beginning of her letter to make a clear statement of the beliefs of the hotel owner?

b Which clause does she then use to express her own feelings?

Exaggerated claims attract customers to products. Customers may then quote these exaggerated claims back at the person who made them if things are not up to scratch.

2 a What claim appears to have been made by the hotel?

b Where might this sort of claim have been made?

3 In a single sentence, summarise the three complaints mentioned by the writer.

4 Now look more closely at the first complaint.

a What adjective is used to make the lack of car parking seem like the hotel's fault?

b Which adjective is used to make the road seem less secure than a car park?

The writer says that she and her family parked half a mile from the hotel. She uses the **passive form** to express this idea. The passive form changes sentence structure in the following way. Instead of saying something like

You made us walk.

the passive takes out the subject of the sentence and produces

We were made to walk.

5 a What does the writer say instead of

Your tiny car park forced us to park half a mile away on a public road.

b Why do you think the writer leaves out the phrase *your tiny car park* in her sentence?

Look again at the following phrase.

After hauling our suitcases to the hotel

6 a *Hauling* is the continuous participle of which verb?

b What does the writer mean to emphasise by choosing this verb?

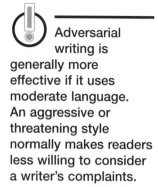
Adversarial writing is generally more effective if it uses moderate language. An aggressive or threatening style normally makes readers less willing to consider a writer's complaints.

Revision booster

Sometimes complaints can seem trivial or silly. Writers may need to emphasise **consequences** in order to show that they are not just being over fussy. You have already looked at the way the writer emphasises the consequences of the hotel not having a larger car park.

7 How does the writer emphasise that badly stocked rooms cause inconvenience?

How did I do?

I know how to analyse adversarial texts. ☐

65: Language of advice

Get started

The following passage is an extract from an article that appeared not long ago in a health magazine. It advises people about the dangers of eating too much salt. The text below is from the start of the article.

Everyone knows we should eat less salt. How do we go about doing it though? Read on, and all will become clear.

You should reduce your intake of pre-packaged food. Most ready meals are packed full of salt. In fact, a recent study found that a popular brand of soup was as salty as sea water. For some reason, manufacturers are not getting the message. They don't seem to be listening. We want your food, but we don't want your salt!

Remember that **pronouns** are words that make reference to nouns. Some words commonly used as pronouns are

we   they   no one   everyone   you

Practice

1 At the start of the passage, a pronoun suggests that the salt issue is widely understood. Which pronoun is used to emphasise this point?

2 Sometimes writers address their readers directly. This is common in advice. Which pronoun makes a direct address at the start of the second paragraph?

3 What pronoun is used in the rest of the passage to make the reader feel included?

4 What pronoun identifies food manufacturers as 'the other side'.

Modal verbs combine with main verbs in the following sorts of ways.

might go   should take   must see   can try   could go

5 a Which modal verb from the list above is used twice in the passage?

b Write down the main verb it combines with on each occasion.

Recall that **imperatives** are created by using the second person of the verb without the subject *you*. The following are examples of imperatives.

Drive *carefully on your way home.*

Stay *calm if you're in an accident.*

Be *careful when you're up the ladder.*

As you can see, they can be used to give friendly advice and instructions.

(6) Where in the passage is an imperative used to give the reader some friendly advice?

You know that adverbial phrases can often be replaced with single adverbs. The adverbial phrase *in fact* can often be replaced with the single adverb *indeed*. Try this with the *chocolate* example below. Unfortunately, this leads a lot of students to spell *in fact* in the following way

infact

This is always wrong.

The writer advises her readers to stay clear of pre-packaged food. This advice is based on the claim that this sort of food is full of salt.

(7) a Which verb is used to emphasise the fact that this kind of food is full of salt?

 b What type of pre-packaged food is used by the writer as evidence for her claims?

 c Often writers will use similes to make their points clearer. What is the food compared to that emphasises its saltiness?

Revision booster

Look at the phrase *in fact* near the middle of the second paragraph. *In fact* is an adverbial phrase used to strengthen a point just made. It is used like this.

I don't like chocolate. **In fact**, *I hate it!*

(8) a What point is about to be strengthened by the use of *in fact* in the passage above?

 b What does the writer provide to strengthen the point?

How did I do?

I know how to examine advice.

✔

☐

66: Explanations

In this unit you will learn
▸ to analyse writing that explains

Get started

In the following extract, a Year 10 student, Rebecca Hanley, explains why she opted for History at the end of Year 9.

> I've always liked history, even in Juniors where you do the Saxons and Romans. I love all the action. There's always something going on. I like studying how people behaved in different centuries. They were so different to us. People had to put up with things that we can't imagine today. Epidemics, witch hunts, famines – it seems impossible from our comfortable position looking back.

Practice

1 a When does the writer say she became interested in history?

   b Which periods of history was she particularly interested in when she was younger?

   c Name three things the writer says that people had to put up with in the past.

Look again at the following two sentences.

I love all the action.

They were so different to us.

The verbs are in different tenses.

2 a Which verbs are used in each sentence?

   b Write down the verb tense used in each of the two sentences.

   c Explain why the writer changes verb tense.

 Rebecca gives the word *History* a capital *H* when she is writing about it as a school subject. At these times she uses it as a proper noun. At other times, she uses the word (with a small *h*) as a common noun simply to refer to the past.

Rebecca goes on to explain why she thinks so few girls at her school do History.

> I think the first reason that girls don't opt for History at our school is because there are no women teachers. Some of my friends would definitely have done it if there had been. The second reason is more important, though. It is because history itself is full of men. Think about it. History is full of male superheroes!

3 a What two reasons does the writer give for girls not doing History at her school?

b What matching pair of three-word noun phrases does the writer use to highlight the fact that she is providing reasons in a logical order?

c Who does the writer say would have done History if there had been women teachers?

d Which adverb indicates she is certain that her statement about her friends is true?

A small number of adverbs can be used to show that a statement already made is about to be modified. One of these adverbs is *however.* Adverbs like *however* are used like this.

Apples contain Vitamin C. Blackcurrants contain more, however.

The statement about apples is modified in the light of the evidence about blackcurrants. Notice how the adverb is sectioned off with a comma.

4 Rebecca uses an adverb in a similar way to this in the extract. Write out the sentence in which an adverb is used in a similar way to *however.*

Imperative sentences are those that use an infinitive form of a verb and omit a subject. For example

Print out a copy.

Tell me again.

Show me the reason.

They are used in this sort of writing to show a kind of friendly directness. Rebecca knows her idea is controversial and she wants the reader to consider it.

5 Write out her imperative sentence.

Rebecca increases the dramatic impact of her idea at the end of her passage.

6 How does she highlight her unusual idea in the closing sentence?

How did I do?

I know how to analyse writing that explains. ✔ ☐

67: Reports

Get started

Read this extract from a report concerning the condition of an outdoor pool in a small Somerset town.

> Considering its age, the town's outdoor pool is in excellent condition. The linings have just been replaced and soon the pump room will be refitted. At the end of the year, work will begin on renovating the downstairs showers. Refurbished last in the early 1980s, these areas must be given attention.

Practice

1 a What area of the pool is about to be refitted?

b When will work begin on the showers?

c When were the showers last attended to?

This is a carefully written report that conveys detail efficiently and with good style. It demonstrates that one way of writing fluently is occasionally to use participle phrases at the beginning of sentences. This creates variety and is a good way of building sentences. Sentences that begin with participle phrases look as follows:

Shaking *its mane, the lion yawned.*   (starting with a continuous participle)

Published *in May, the book has sold well.*   (starting with a past participle)

Notice that these participle phrases are sectioned off with a comma, and that they should always relate to the subject of the verb.

2 In the extract above, which are the two participle phrases used at the start of sentences?

a a continuous participle

b a past participle

This report is largely concerned with *what* is being done *when*. Time relations can be indicated by writers through verb tense and choice of adverb. For example, the present perfect tense is used to describe actions recently completed.

3 a Which repair job has already been completed?

b What adverb (a single word) is used to show that the repair happened very recently?

c Which verb tense is used to indicate the time of this recent repair?

d Which verb is added to the infinitives *be* and *begin* to indicate future time?

Look at these clauses.

The roads have been mended

The house has just been extended

The pipes will be relaid

All these clauses are **passive**. They are extremely common in reports and other forms of formal writing. They are an excellent way of communicating what needs to be done. They do not concern themselves with *who* will do it.

Read the clauses again. In none of them is the reader told *who* will do the mending, extending and relaying. This is not because the writer wishes to hide these details. It is because they are less important than the jobs to be done.

Notice the structure of these passive clauses.

noun phrase + form of the verb *be* + perfect participle

There are three passive clauses in the swimming pool text. The first one is

the linings have just been replaced   (the reader doesn't know who replaced them)

> Use passives clauses to communicate a serious and efficient tone when needed.

4 Write down the other two passive clauses.

Prefixes are letter units used at the beginnings of words that have common meanings. Here are some examples.

im	means *not*	e.g. *impossible*	means	*not possible*
super	means *greater*	e.g. *superpower*	means	*greater power*
pre	means *before*	e.g. *prehistoric*	means	*before history*

5 What (two-letter) prefix meaning *again* is used at the start of four words in the passage?

Revision booster

Remember that modal verbs are used before infinitives to indicate things like probability, possibility and uncertainty.

6 Which individual modal verb is used in the final sentence of the passage to suggest obligation and urgency?

How did I do?

I know how to assess structure in reports. ✔ ☐

68: Promotional writing

In this unit you will learn
▸ to explore promotional writing

Get started

Read the text that follows. It is designed to promote a housing development.

> Shoebury sits proudly at the head of the Thames estuary. For centuries, she has welcomed visitors to these islands. In more recent times, the town has had a crucial role in our defence against invaders. During the middle of the Victorian era, a mighty garrison was settled. The soldiers have left now, but their superb buildings remain.

Practice

1
  a Where exactly is Shoebury?

  b When was the garrison first settled?

  c What is left of the garrison?

Promotional writing attempts to be as positive as it can possibly be about what it describes. It needs, after all, to have a very direct impact on its readership. All promotional writing, at some point, aims to convince a reader that its advertised product is worth buying.

2 In the first sentence of the text,

  a what verb is used to suggest calm and dignity?

  b what adverb suggests that Shoebury can boast about its position?

Estuaries are often (metaphorically) described as the *mouths* of rivers.

3
  a What metaphor is used to describe the position on the Thames estuary?

  b Why do you think this metaphor was chosen?

Personal pronouns are used to refer to nouns. Look at the following examples.

(she/her) the woman   (they/them) these builders   (it) this stone

Notice that, as a very common rule, people are referred to by the pronouns *he* and *she*. *Things* are referred to by the pronoun *it*.

Shoebury, like a stone, is a *thing*.

4
  a What pronoun is used to refer to Shoebury in the second sentence?

  b What is the effect of this pronoun?

  c What other non-living thing is sometimes referred to by this pronoun?

Three-word noun phrases are a common descriptive technique. They consist of a determiner, an adjective and a noun. Look at the following examples.

these great towers

this tremendous idea

a stunning conclusion

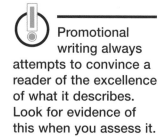 Promotional writing always attempts to convince a reader of the excellence of what it describes. Look for evidence of this when you assess it.

5 Three noun phrases, identical in structure to those above, appear in the text. They have been carefully constructed to suggest the importance of Shoebury and the soldiers who once lived there.

a Which noun phrase indicates the vital part played by the town in stopping invaders?

b Which noun phrase suggests the great power of the garrison?

c Which noun phrase is used to describe the wonderful architecture still standing?

Look at the start of the second, third and fourth sentences of the text. They all begin with adverbial phrases that are sectioned off with commas. These adverbial phrases all tell the reader *when* things occurred. Like adverbs, adverbial phrases can often be moved around in sentences to create different effects. Consider the following example.

For millions of years, dinosaurs ruled the Earth.

Dinosaurs ruled the Earth for millions of years.

6 a Rewrite the second sentence in the passage with the adverbial phrase moved to the end.

b Repeat this process for the third and fourth sentences.

Now read the whole of the rewritten text to yourself. It should still make good sense but notice how the style has been damaged by moving the adverbial phrases. The text will now seem much more like a list. Remember this effect in your own writing.

Revision booster

This promotional text is anxious to establish that Shoebury has a long and distinguished history. Evidence of a dignified history is often important for something that is new, such as a housing development.

7 a Which two-word phrase describes Shoebury's importance over hundreds of years?

b Which phrase recalls an important period in British history?

How did I do?

I know how to explore promotional writing.

69: Structuring an argument

In this unit you will learn
▶ to structure convincing arguments

Get started

Read the following introduction to an article about graffiti.

> Some people say that kids who tag walls with graffiti are artists. Others have argued that taggers are expressing their rage against the adult world. A minority believes that tag bandits are part of the human tradition of cave decoration. I can't agree with any of this, however. To my mind, these tag mites are just bored attention seekers.

A crucial part of any effective argument is to *acknowledge the other side*. You have to show that you know what other people think. This gives the impression that you have considered all the arguments and have come up with the best ones.

The writer of this extract spends her first three sentences acknowledging the opinions of people who disagree with her about graffiti artists.

Practice

1 In a single sentence, summarise the three opinions that the writer says other people have of graffiti artists.

Look at the adverb *however* in the fourth sentence. It is an extremely useful word to use in arguments. It shows that there is a contrast between one thing and another, for example, your ideas and someone else's.

You think this or that. I don't agree, however.

When it is used in this way, the word *however* needs to be separated from the other words in the sentence with commas.

However, I don't agree.

I don't, however, agree.

I don't agree, however.

The sentences all mean the same. Where you put *however* is your decision. It is all a part of your personal writing style.

2 Write out two new versions of the extract's fourth sentence, changing only the position of the adverb *however*. Use the three sentences above as your guide. Remember to use the correct sentence punctuation each time.

Writers often use little phrases that direct readers to their own way of thinking. These phrases make it clear that the writer is now expressing a personal opinion, rather than summarising somebody else's. Examples of these short phrases are

In my opinion *To my way of thinking* *In my view* *From my viewpoint*

Notice that the determiner *my* is used each time to signal that it is the writer's *personal* opinion that is about to be expressed.

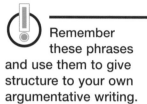

Remember these phrases and use them to give structure to your own argumentative writing.

3 a What phrase, similar to those above, is used in the extract?

b Write a whole sentence beginning with one of the above phrases. Separate the phrase from the rest of the sentence with a comma.

Writers don't always want (or need) to say *exactly* who is responsible for an argument, an idea or an action. When this happens they often use noun phrases (usually at the beginning of sentences) like this

A majority *now believes that the climate is changing.*

Many people *think that it's time for a hosepipe ban.*

Most experts *agree that babies need calcium.*

The *agent* of the action is left unclear at best. It is the *argument* that is important, not the person or people making it.

4 The writer of the passage on the left leaves three agents unclear at the start of the first three sentences of her article. Write down the noun phrases (either a single word or two words in these cases) that she uses to describe the agents making the arguments.

Remember reference chains. They are chains of nouns, pronouns or noun phrases that refer to the same thing. They hold texts together (they give texts **cohesion**). They are also used by writers to express opinions. After all, the name we give something often reveals what we feel about it. At the start of the article in this unit, for example, graffiti artists are called *kids who tag walls with graffiti*.

5 a Write down all the other noun references used to describe these kids.

b What do these names suggest about the writer's attitude towards them?

How did I do?

I can structure convincing arguments.

70: Persuasive techniques (1)

> In this unit you will learn
> ▶ to understand persuasive techniques

Get started

This extract is from a letter recently sent out by a primary school. It persuades parents to get involved in the school fair.

> Are you fit? Do you have a sense of humour? Can you give up a couple of hours of your time for a very worthy cause next Saturday afternoon? If you can, you could be just the person we are looking for. We need enthusiastic and energetic people like you to help with our school fair.

Remember that the personal pronouns are

I/me   you   he/him   she/her   it   we/us   they/them

Practice

1 a Which personal pronoun is used throughout the passage to address the reader?

b Why do you think persuasive writing often refers to the reader in this way?

Rhetorical questions are another common feature of persuasive writing. These are questions that do not need a reply. The reader is expected to ask the questions of him- or herself. In the case of this letter, the answers can only be either *yes* or *no*.

2 a How many rhetorical questions are asked in this extract?

b How would most people wish to answer the opening two questions?

c What effect does the writer hope this will have on the answer to the final question?

Now look again at the final rhetorical question. It contains three phrases that are important for the persuasive impact of the letter. The phrases are

a couple of hours

your time

a very worthy cause

3 a Helpers at the fair are going to have to give up their own time. How is the first phrase designed to make them feel about this fact?

b What does the second phrase show about the writer's attitude to the time being given?

c In what way is the third phrase persuasive?

 Persuasive writing often flatters its readers.

You have already seen how the first two rhetorical questions are designed to lead readers into answers that are flattering. This light-hearted flattery continues at the end of the letter when the writer assumes that the reader is a certain type of person.

4 Which two adjectives used in the final sentence make an assumption that flatters the reader?

Persuasive writing often flatters its readers. In addition, it sometimes emphasises the neediness of the writer. One way of doing this, of course, is to ask direct questions of the reader. Another is through the verbs used to express what is wanted.

5 a Which four-word phrase used in the fourth sentence suggests the writer is searching?

b Write down the pronoun and verb used at the start of the final sentence.

c What is the final verb used in the extract?

Look at the words and phrases you have extracted from the text for this task. See how they communicate a very clear message indeed.

Revision booster

Determiners are words like

my   his   the   their   a

They are used before nouns and noun phrases, like this

a school fair

the school fair

any school fair

6 a What determiner is used for the *school fair* in the extract?

b What does the determiner suggest about the writer's attitude towards the fair?

How did I do?

I understand persuasive techniques.

71: Persuasive techniques (2)

In this unit you will learn
▶ to understand persuasive techniques

Get started

This extract comes from the beginning of a website article by Cara Stratton.

> *I live in a friendly coastal town. It's a lovely place to be, except that it's abused every weekend and bank holiday by a single unwelcome visitor. The visitor's name? Litter!*

Practice

1 a Which two adjectives are used early on by Cara to make her town seem attractive?

b Which one word explains how her attractive town is treated by litter?

c Explain how the importance of the word *litter* is emphasised by Cara.

 Rhetorical questions are a good way for writers to bring readers round to their own way of thinking. That's why these sorts of questions are important in persuasive and argumentative writing.

Writers ask **rhetorical questions** to involve their readers in a sort of discussion. Examples are

Why does our town look so scruffy?

And the most serious problem in my school?

What can we do about dog mess?

Writers pretend to imagine that rhetorical questions come from readers. That's why you can always put the phrase *I hear you ask* after any rhetorical question. Try it with the examples above.

Of course, if writers don't answer their own rhetorical questions then nobody will. Cara Stratton does choose to answer her question in the extract above.

2 Write down Cara's rhetorical question and the answer she provides.

3 Give your own answers to the three rhetorical questions above.

If you think hard about it, only living things (like dogs and people) can truly be friendly, not things that are inanimate, like stones, books and towns. The same is true of visitors. Visitors need to be alive, otherwise they're not really visitors.

Writers often imagine that inanimate things are alive. It is sometimes an effective thing to do. When they do this it is called **personification**. Cara does it twice.

4 Complete the following sentences to show this.

    a The town is personified by calling it ...

    b Litter is personified by calling it ...

Personification makes the town seem more than just a collection of buildings. And it makes litter seem more than just a mess of paper bags and tin cans.

5 Explain the effect of personification in the introduction to Cara's article.

Cara finishes her article about litter in the following way.

> Litter is a lout, a hooligan, a yob, whose frequent visits are unwanted. How can we rid ourselves of this pest? We need to work together and there's no end to what we can do. Tell people who drop litter not to. Pick up litter yourself. Write to the council. Go into fast-food joints and tell the manager loudly that the pavement outside is covered in rubbish bearing the company name. And please, please, please – don't ever drop litter yourself. Your town is a friend – don't abuse it.

6   a Which three words in the first sentence are used to personify litter?

    b How does this use of personification make Cara's feelings about litter clear?

    c What effect does she hope her rhetorical question will have on the reader?

Look again at the extract above.

7   a How many things does Cara include in her list of things to do?

    b Why does she include such a variety of things in this list?

    c How does she emphasise the importance of readers not dropping litter themselves?

    d What is the effect of Cara's use of personification in the last sentence?

Revision booster

Write an introduction to an article about a problem local to you. Use Cara's article as a guide. Use personification and include a rhetorical question with an answer.

How did I do?

I understand persuasive techniques.

✔
☐

72: Persuasion

In this unit you will learn
- ▶ to comment on persuasive techniques

Get started

The following extract is part of a letter written by a Year 9 pupil in response to a recent Key Stage 3 test question. The question asked students to write a letter to local people warning them that their sports centre was about to close.

Dear Friends,

You may have heard that our local sports centre is about to close. The closure of this centre would be a disaster. It is used by all members of our community for fun and leisure. Mothers take their children to the crèche and have a coffee while they play. Elderly people go to the keep fit classes every afternoon. Local students attend clubs and activities at the centre that are available nowhere else. Do you really think it would be a good idea to lose all this? Can you imagine the consequences?

We are always being told that we should exercise more. How are we to do this if our main exercise centre closes? We will all become overweight and unfit. It is said that teenagers are a problem but they are fine around here. Why? They are no problem because they have somewhere to go. Who knows what will happen if their main source of entertainment disappears. Think of all the people who will be thrown out of work if the sports centre closes. It will be devastating.

Practice

1
a Who is the audience for this letter?

b At the very start of the letter, how does the writer try get the audience on his side?

Look at the first sentence. The main idea in this sentence is picked up and developed in the second sentence. We can trace this by looking at related words and new vocabulary.

2
a Which word in the first sentence is *closure* similar to?

b Which phrase in the first sentence is *this centre* related to?

c Which key word then moves the second sentence beyond the ideas of the first sentence?

ⓘ Persuasive texts need to provide good evidence in support of their main arguments.

3
a Summarise the main idea of the third sentence (beginning *It is used ...*).

b What four groups of people are then used as evidence to support this main idea?

At the end of the first paragraph, the writer asks the reader to imagine what will happen if the sports centre closes. He then uses the second paragraph to answer his own question.

4 Summarise three of the things the writer believes will happen if the sports centre is shut down.

5 Early in the letter, the writer says that the closure of the centre will be a disaster.

    a What very similar phrase does this link up with at the end of the extract?

    b What is the point of repeating these similar phrases?

Writers of persuasive texts often exaggerate in order to emphasise what they want to say. This is a good idea so long as it is not overdone. For example, it would not convince anyone to say that the closure of the sports centre would lead to gang warfare.

6 a Which single word is used to exaggerate the idea that people will become unfit?

    b Which four-word phrase is used to exaggerate the way people might lose their jobs?

Passive sentences and phrases take the following form.

We are always being told to exercise more.

It is said that teenagers are a problem ...

We don't know from these sentences who it is that tells the writer to exercise or who it is that says teenagers are a problem. This is not because the writer wants to keep it a secret. No one in particular says these things. They are just things which are generally said. Using the passive form is an excellent way of expressing these general comments.

The passive is formed by leaving out the person or thing that does the acting or doing.

The government tells us to exercise becomes *We are told to exercise*

People say teenagers are a problem becomes *It is said that teenagers are a problem*

7 Make the following sentences passive.

    a *The coach has asked us to play   We have been asked ...*

    b *The ambulance took me to hospital   I was taken ...*

    c *They have beaten us   We have ...*

    d *He knocked me on the head   I was ...*

How did I do?

I can comment on persuasive techniques.

73: Journalism

In this unit you will learn
▶ to consider features of journalism

Get started

The extract below is taken from an article that recently appeared in a local newspaper in the south of England. The passage comes from the beginning of the news story.

> *The Echo can today reveal that a key committee on our local council has just spent over £370,000 on a 'fact finding' mission to Moscow. Well-placed sources confirm that the Public Transport Group visited the Russian capital to examine transport systems. The Echo is also able to disclose that the five councillors on the committee stayed for three nights in the luxury Shangri La hotel.*

The word *can* is one of a group of modal verbs that modify other verbs. In common with other modal verbs, *can* is used to modify the infinitive form of the main verb. It is used in the following familiar way.

*She **can** speak Hungarian.*

This modal verb can generally be replaced by the phrase *is able to.* Try it with the sentence about Hungarian above.

Newspapers often use the modal verb *can.* It suggests that after lots of investigative work they are finally able to tell their readers the facts about something important. This technique produces sentences such as the following one.

*The Globe **can** confirm that Snow Patrol will perform live in the town next year.*

*The Globe **is able to** confirm that Snow Patrol will perform live in the town next year.*

Practice

1 The *Echo* introduces two of its sentences using the method explained above.

a Write down the start of each sentence that uses the technique.

b Which main verb is modified in each of the two sentences?

Notice that the technique makes the story *belong* to the newspaper. For example, everyone may well already know that *Snow Patrol* are visiting next year. By *revealing* or *confirming* this news, however, the journalists write as if nobody knew it but themselves. You can see better how this works by completely removing the clause that contains the modal. This will produce

Snow Patrol will perform live in the town next year.

Notice that the newspaper no longer advertises its own part in the story.

Look again at this effect by doing the same thing to the two sentences from the *Echo*.

Newspapers use **sources**. These are people 'in the know' who may be friends of the journalist or who may simply be invented. The word *sources* is a very important one. It allows newspapers to say that someone has told them a story without having to say who it is. Detailed noun phrases can be built up around these *sources* (and related nouns) to suggest their importance and reliability.

Reliable sources

Sources close to the government

Friends of the victim

Close friends of the Home Secretary

Sources within the company

All these phrases suggest that an important person is telling the story. But they avoid saying exactly who that important person is. This protects the source and (in the case of less serious newspapers) enables journalists to make stories up.

2 Write down the (three-word) noun phrase in the *Echo* article that refers to the sources used by the newspaper.

The article from the *Echo* suggests that the councillors have done something wrong. It does not say this outright. Newspapers often imply things in this way. They avoid saying things directly in case it gets them into trouble. This forces them to suggest and hint.

Look at the verb *reveal* in the first sentence. If you replace this verb with another one like *report* then the feeling of the sentence changes.

3 a What is the verb *reveal* meant to suggest?

b What is the adjective used to describe the hotel in which the councillors stayed?

c What is being suggested (or *implied*) by this adjective?

Things can be implied by quoting the person who is being criticised. If an important hospital goes bankrupt, a journalist might write this.

The government believes the hospital has a 'minor funding difficulty'.

The quotation implies that, in the face of the evidence, the government is out of touch.

4 a What quotation is used in the *Echo* article?

b Who is supposed to have made the statement in the quotation?

c What are readers meant to think about the statement?

How did I do?

I can consider features of journalism.

74: Biography

Get started

This extract is taken from one of a series of biographical profiles (real life stories) published by a Sunday paper. The passage forms an introduction to the story of William Brown, one of the last British rubber plantation owners to leave Malaysia. At the time of the article, he had returned to Britain to retire. The passage begins with the journalist arriving at William Brown's flat.

> It is raining hard as I arrive at William Brown's small flat. I knock on his door and he welcomes me in out of the flood. He is smiling from ear to ear.
>
> "It rained like this every lunchtime in Malaya," he says. "You could set your watch by it."
>
> William Brown left Malaysia (he still calls it by its colonial name, Malaya) five years ago. He had lived there for almost sixty years. During his time there, he witnessed a world war and the collapse of empire. He saw civil unrest and great social change.
>
> "I was playing cricket once against a team from Ipoh," he says. "The opposition captain told me life had improved in Britain. He said I should go back. I told him I was staying. I have had a very happy life. I have done everything I wanted."

Setting a scene can be as important in biography as in fiction. Writers often use the weather to help them set the mood at the beginning of a text.

Practice

1 a What does the writer focus on to set the scene at the start of her article?

b What noun does she use in her second sentence to dramatise the weather?

The reader's first impression of William Brown is gained by something he is doing.

2 a What is William Brown doing?

b What impression does the reader immediately get of him?

Cohesion between paragraphs is an important feature of all texts. Cohesion refers to the way texts hold together and are developed.

3 a What do the first and second paragraphs have in common?

b How is the subject matter moved on by the second paragraph?

People on the page can be brought to life (or **characterised**) by providing the reader with small details about their personalities.

! Small details can tell readers lots about character. Look for them carefully.

④ Malaysia changed its name from Malaya nearly fifty years ago. The writer characterises William Brown by telling the reader that he still calls it by its colonial name. What impression does this small detail give of William Brown?

⑤ a What game does the writer refer to in the passage?

b What impression does this detail give of William Brown?

Good biographical writing may include a range of verb tenses. This is one way of avoiding a repetitive string of past tense verbs.

He lived *in Malaya. He* owned *a rubber plantation. He* played *cricket. He* returned *to England.*

The writer of the profile avoids this trap. One of her techniques is to use the present tense to talk about past events. This can create the sense of something happening that is immediate and present to the reader.

⑥ Look at the first paragraph.

a Which two present continuous verbs (two words in length) does the writer use?

b Find three simple present tense verbs (each one word long) that are used.

Recall the following details of verb construction.

● The present perfect is formed with *have* or *has* before the perfect participle.

● The past perfect is formed with *had* before the perfect participle.

● The past continuous is formed with *was* or *were* before the continuous participle.

⑦ Look at the third and fourth paragraphs of the passage and find the following. Note that each of the verbs you are looking for is formed from the combination of two words.

a two verbs used in the present perfect tense

b two verbs used in the past perfect tense

c two verbs used in the past continuous tense

Look at the way each of these tenses is used in the text. Notice that they help to express time in a very specific way.

How did I do?

I can consider features of biography. ✔ ☐

75: Viewpoint in non-fiction

In this unit you will learn
- ▶ to analyse viewpoint in non-fiction

Get started

In his book, *The Sculpted Gods*, Jared Seaton describes his adventures as a mountaineer. In this extract, he describes a visit to Mount Kinabulu, on the island of Borneo.

> Mount Kinabulu is indeed a heavenly sight. It presses into the blue cloth of the Borneo sky like the rocky muscle of some sculpted god. To ascend a mountain like this is to embrace nature at its most rugged. We knelt at its feet. We knew our embrace must be worshipful.

Remember that an adjective is a descriptive word used to provide extra detail about a noun. In this extract, Jared's use of adjectives provides the reader with an excellent understanding of his view of Mount Kinabulu.

Practice

 Look closely at the adjectives and verbs chosen by a writer. They can reveal lots to a careful reader.

1
  a What two adjectives (used in the first and the last sentences) show that Jared has a religious sort of respect for the mountain?

  b What two adjectives (used in the middle of the passage) remind the reader that the mountain is made of rock?

  c Jared sees the mountain as something both solid and divine. What noun phrase (in this case an adjective plus a noun) is used at the end of the second sentence to express this point of view?

Verbs are words that express actions. Jared's use of verbs in this extract reveals as much about his viewpoint as his use of adjectives.

2
  a The verb *ascend* is often used to describe the journey of the soul after death. Why do you think Jared uses it to describe his expedition?

  b Why does Jared emphasise the action of kneeling at the end of the passage?

You already know that the same word (for example, *stone* or *fire*) can be used as both a verb and a noun.

3
  a What word is used twice in the last three sentences, first as a verb and then as a noun?

  b What does the use of this word suggest about Jared's feelings towards the mountain?

Later in his book, Jared describes the journey up Kinabulu. He recalls an incident involving a member of his team.

> I had noticed one or two things that concerned me. I'd seen a provision bag littering the camp site after we packed away. I'd also noticed the heads knocked off some of the flowers on the path. I'd heard swearing, something I would not tolerate on this sacred mountain. My instinct pointed to Alanis as the source of this evil but I had no proof. Then I saw her light a fire on unprotected ground. I flew into a rage. She was 'a devil in paradise' I told her. That night she left our camp and I never saw her again.

4　a　In a single sentence, summarise the three things that Jared *suspects* Alanis of.

　　b　What does Jared's concern with these matters indicate about his personality?

> Two noun phrases in this passage remind us directly of Jared's religious view of the expedition. One of them describes the mountain and one of them relates to Alanis.

5　What are the two noun phrases?

Revision booster

Elsewhere in Jared Seaton's book, the reader discovers that Alanis was on her first mountaineering expedition.

6　a　How might this alter the reader's view of Alanis' behaviour?
　　b　How might this affect the reader's view of the way Jared treats Alanis?

How did I do?

I can analyse viewpoint in non-fiction.　✔ ☐

76: Point of view (1)

In this unit you will learn
▶ to interpret point of view

Get started

This extract from an article about stage schools appeared recently in a national newspaper. The author is a journalist called Penny Boynton.

> *Stage schools have been around for many years now. In their early days, they catered only for children of the well to do. They were really no more than finishing schools where wealthy children were sent to have their speech and deportment refined. The rich kids who went to these places could afford to waste their time prancing around in leggings and polishing their vowels. Stage schools turned spoilt brats into unbearably spoilt brats.*

Look carefully at the nouns and noun phrases used by a writer throughout a piece of writing. They will often tell you lots about the way a writer feels towards a subject. In this article, for instance, Penny Boynton describes the basic noun phrase *stage schools* in the following ways.

Stage schools   they   They   finishing schools   these places   Stage schools

These nouns are called a **reference chain**. In other words, all the nouns, pronouns and noun phrases in the chain refer to the same thing. Reference chains hold texts together (without endless repetitions of the same nouns or pronouns like *they*) and they give a reader clues about writer attitude. In this case, the writer's attitude towards *finishing schools* and *these places* does not seem very positive.

Practice

1 a Make your own reference chain of noun phrases (just noun phrases this time) that are used to refer to the children who used to go to stage school. You should find five phrases to make up your chain.

   b What does your reference chain suggest to you about Penny Boynton's feelings towards the children she describes?

   c What is your own reaction to the author's opinions?

2 Look at the author's choice of the verbs *prancing* and *polishing*. What do these verbs suggest about the children at stage school?

3 The author makes it clear early on in the passage that she is not talking about stage schools as they are now. Write down the four-word phrase (beginning with a preposition) that makes it clear she is talking about the past.

Remember that adverbial phrases can move around in sentences. The phrase you identified in question 3 has been used at the start of a sentence to provide variety.

4 a Rewrite the second sentence by moving the adverbial phrase to the end.

  b Now reread the first three sentences of the extract. What did the writer avoid by putting an adverbial phrase at the start of the second sentence?

Penny Boynton's article continues a little later in the following way.

Stage schools have now changed. They are centres of excellence where children from all backgrounds can work together on constructive and stimulating projects. They provide excellent training for every child.

5 Which single adverb, used in the first sentence, provides a contrast with the *early days*?

Revision booster

6 a Make a reference chain for the stage schools in this passage. It should contain two pronouns and two noun phrases.

  b How has the writer changed the way she describes stage schools?

7 Find three adjectives (two that describe *projects* and one that describes *training*) that demonstrate the writer's change in attitude.

8 Look at the determiners used before the nouns *backgrounds* and *child*. How do these determiners emphasise the difference (in the writer's eyes) between stage schools now and in the past?

How did I do?

I can interpret point of view. ✔ ☐

77: Point of view (2)

Get started

This extract is from an article that was published in a national newspaper shortly after the end of the 2006 football World Cup.

> In the end we came nowhere. After all those miles of newsprint. After the hope and the expectation. After the endless discussions about tactics and formations. After the boasts and promises, all our footballers could do was defend their way to defeat.

When the writer says *we,* she means the England football team who didn't do as well in the World Cup as many had hoped and expected.

Practice

1 In no more than a sentence, sum up the way this writer feels about England's World Cup campaign.

Look again at the very first sentence. It is made up of two parts. Normally the second part *we came nowhere* would come before the first part *in the end* to make the sentence

We came nowhere in the end.

2 Identify the separate sections in the following sentences and then exchange them to create the same effect as the opening sentence of the extract.

a I'll be able to speak when you've finished chattering.

b It was absolutely no good after all that.

Moving segments to the beginning of sentences can draw them to a reader's attention. In the first sentence in question 2, for example, attention is drawn to the *chattering.*

3 Why does the writer of the article want readers to notice the phrase *in the end* at the start of her first sentence?

Writers can alter the normal order of words and phrases to create impact and effect.

The remaining sentences in the extract all begin with the word *After.* Look again at the third sentence

After the hope and the expectation.

The writer has chosen to write another unusual sentence. This one is unusual because it does not contain a verb. There is nothing else in the sentence to explain what it means. The meaning is only explained when a verb is included.

*After the hope and the expectation, we **came** nowhere.*

4 Add a verb and supporting words to each of the following sentences so that their meanings are explained.

a *After all those miles of newsprint*

b *After the endless discussions about tactics and formations*

5 The writer is suggesting that the meanings of these sentences do not actually need to be spelled out. Why does she suggest this?

6
a Why does the writer use the phrase *miles of newsprint*?

b Write down one word used by the writer to describe the talk about tactics and formations.

c What does this word suggest about her attitude towards tactics?

d According to the writer, what did the footballers do before the tournament?

7 The writer uses a verb near the end of the passage to suggest the way the England team went down to defeat.

a Which verb does she use?

b How do you think she would have preferred England to lose?

Revision booster

The headline of this article was

End of the World?

8
a What does this phrase suggest about the way fans saw England's defeat?
b What does the question mark suggest the writer is prepared to ask?
c How do you think the writer would answer her own question?

How did I do?

✔

I know how to analyse writer attitude. ☐

78: Purpose and viewpoint

In this unit you will learn

▶ to comment on purpose and viewpoint

Get started

This is an extract from a holiday brochure advertising destinations in the Arabian Gulf.

The Pearl of the Gulf

Bahrain, our small, friendly island, just off the coast of Saudi Arabia in the sparkling Arabian Gulf, must be one of the most interesting and exciting places on Earth. It's a rainbow of contrasts: between the sea and the land; between desert and garden; between the modern and the traditional. Come and visit.

Your first port of call, whether you arrive by boat or by plane, is our capital, Manama. This modern, cosmopolitan city boasts fine hotels and luxurious shopping malls that rival those of New York, London or Paris. Every international brand is represented here. If you don't want to stay inside, try shopping in our traditional Arab souks. Gold, leather and finely woven carpets can all be found in these busy street markets at bargain prices. When you want a rest from shopping, stop for something to eat. Our restaurants, like our shops, are second to none. We offer a range of food, from five star cuisine served in the most refined surroundings to tasty kebabs served off bustling street stalls. Don't miss our cinemas, museums and regular outdoor entertainments either. Come and enjoy.

Some of our guests love Manama so much that they never leave. Outside the capital, though, the more adventurous will find plenty to do. Walk up Jabal Dukhan, our highest peak, and admire the sun setting over the misty desert. Marvel at the mysterious burial mounds left by Bahrain's early Dilmun inhabitants many centuries ago. Relax on any one of our glorious, deserted beaches and while away the afternoon listening to the gentle lapping of the surf. Come and discover.

Whatever you want, you'll find it here. There's a world in our island. Come and see.

Practice

1
a Which word in the title of this article is used to make Bahrain sound precious?

b Write down four adjectives from the first sentence that are used to describe Bahrain.

c What is the effect of using the word 'rainbow'?

2 Look at the overall effect of the first paragraph.

a What impression is the writer trying to create of Bahrain?

The purpose of a text is the reason it was written.

b What is the purpose of this piece of writing?

3 In the first paragraph, the writer claims that Bahrain contains a mix of the 'modern and the traditional'. What contrasts are there in the second paragraph between the new and the old?

4 a At the beginning of the second paragraph, the writer claims that Manama has excellent facilities. Write down two phrases that are used to support this claim.

  b What verb is used in the second sentence to suggest that Manama is very proud of its hotels and malls?

5 a Write down the two different words used to describe the street markets and street stalls.

  b What impression of the streets is the writer trying to create with these two words?

6 In the third paragraph, how does the writer describe the people who leave Manama?

7 a Write down three places that these people can go to.

  b Which three verbs are used to make these places seem interesting and attractive?

8 Explain how this paragraph as a whole picks up on the 'rainbow' idea used earlier.

Revision booster

The words *our* and *us* are used throughout this article.

9 What effect is created by using these words?

10 Explain how the last sentence of the first paragraph connects with the opening of the second paragraph.

11 The endings of each paragraph are very similar. What impact is the writer trying to create by ending the paragraphs like this?

How did I do?

I know how to comment on purpose and viewpoint.

☐ ✔

79: Fact and opinion

In this unit you will learn
▶ to present information

Get started

A school near Plymouth recently arranged an Open Day for the parents and carers of Year 7 pupils. A student from Year 7 called Tim Harris was asked to write a letter home to provide information about the day.

> You may already know that the Year 7 Open Day will be taking place on Tuesday, 6th April. It is intended as an opportunity for parents and carers to come into the school and actually see what their children do on a daily basis. There will be exhibitions of students' work, demonstrations of activities and chances for parents to become involved in a variety of events. The day will begin with an introduction from Mrs Cooke at 9.30 in Room P4. Parents are welcome to stay for as long or as short a time as they wish. We do hope you will be able to attend. It's going to be an excellent day.

Practice

Informative writing must contain useful facts.

1
  a Which two hard facts does Tim Harris provide in this letter about date and time?

  b What fact does Tim provide about where the Open Day will start off?

Opinions can often provide interest to informative writing.

2 Tim offers an opinion at the end of his letter. What kind of day does he believe people will have?

There are two important ways of expressing uncertainty in language. One way, of course, is by asking a direct question.

Did you know I have your credit card?

The other way is by using one of the modal verbs you've worked with in previous units. Modal verbs are often used to *suggest*. They are *less direct* than questions and they are often used in formal writing.

You may know I have your credit card.

3 In which sentence does Tim use a modal verb in the way shown here?

Modal verbs express uncertainty. They can be used in texts to do this either with or instead of direct questions.

Writers base their information around nouns. After all, it is *things* that readers of the information need to know about. Nouns can obviously provide information on their own (or with a single determiner like *a*). For example

a display

a presentation

but these nouns can be given detail and depth by using prepositions to expand them into longer noun phrases.

a display of colour

a presentation of dances from around the world

activities for everyone

Tim Harris used the prepositions *of, for* and *from* in a variety of noun phrases. One of his noun phrases is

opportunity for parents

4 Find three other noun phrases like the one above in the letter.

You have already looked at the way modal verbs can be used to express uncertainty. The verb *do* can be placed in front of an infinitive (just as a modal verb is) to express not uncertainty but emphasis.

*I **do** want to go.   Those shoes **do** look fantastic.   They **do** regret their actions.*

5 a Write down the sentence in the text where Tim Harris does this.

  b How is he trying to make his audience feel?

Tim Harris is describing a future event (the Open Day) so it is not surprising that he often uses the simple future tense in his letter. In other words, he places *will* before an infinitive form to make combinations like *will be* and *will begin*. The future, however, can be expressed in other ways. One of them is by taking the continuous participle (*ing* form) of *go* and adding it to the preposition *to* and an infinitive.

going to dance   going to make   going to build

6 Write down the sentence in which Tim Harris expresses future time in this way.

How did I do?

I can present information.   ☑ ☐

80: Shakespeare's language

In this unit you will learn
▶ to explore Shakespeare's use of language

Get started

The following lines come from a play by William Shakespeare called *Richard II*.
They are an extract from a speech made by the King's uncle, John of Gaunt.
He is talking with great enthusiasm about England.

> This royal throne of kings, this sceptred isle,
>
> This earth of majesty, this seat of Mars,   [Mars – God of War]
>
> This other Eden, demi-paradise,
>
> This fortress built by nature for herself
>
> Against infection and the hand of war,
>
> This happy breed of men, this little world,
>
> This precious stone set in the silver sea,
>
> Which serves it in the office of a wall,
>
> Or as a moat defensive to a house,
>
> Against the envy of less happier lands;
>
> This blessed plot, this Earth, this realm, this England.

Practice

In the first line of this speech, Gaunt describes England with the noun phrase
this sceptred isle. He creates the image of England holding a royal sceptre or
staff. The image is similar to those of Britannia or the Statue of Liberty.

1 What other two noun phrases in the first two lines portray England in this royal
or regal way?

Gaunt also portrays England as heavenly. It is called a *demi-paradise*, a place
that is close to being heaven.

2 Find two other phrases that connect England with heavens and the gods.

These lines were written three hundred years before the invention of planes and
long-range missiles. The sea around Britain protected it from attack.

3 a What word is used in the fourth line to suggest that England is a safe haven?

b The sea is compared to two protective structures. What are they?

5 Look at the way the noun phrases *the fields* and *the air* combine with other words. How do these combinations indicate that this London is clearly not a modern city?

6 Wordsworth lists a number of things that are found in the countryside. He makes a comparison between the beauty of the country and the calm splendour of London. Which three things does he list in a row, which remind the reader of the country?

He refers to the way the sun shines on the beautiful features of the countryside. It reminds him of the way the sun is rising over Westminster Bridge.

7 The poet doesn't use the adverbial phrase *in the morning* to describe the morning sun rising over the countryside.

a What (four-word) phrase does he use instead?

b Which single word in this phrase reminds us of the majesty mentioned earlier?

c Which single word in the phrase personifies the sun as a man?

Remember that personification is the skill of making non-living things seem alive or human. It is the art of breathing life into inanimate objects. Wordsworth does this when he imagines the sun as a man, rising over the countryside and bathing the rocks in light. You have also seen how he describes the city as if it is dressed in splendid clothes.

The poet personifies the river as having a *sweet will,* almost as if it can decide what to do with itself.

8 a Which other single word personifies the river?

b The houses are personified too. What do they seem to be doing?

c On the last line of the poem, what does Wordsworth imagine the city has?

Revision booster

9 Wordsworth is unimpressed by those who could just pass by the scene he witnesses. As he watches the river gliding by, which single word sums up his *own* feeling of peace and quiet?

Canaletto's painting of Westminster Bridge indicates the kind of view Wordsworth would have enjoyed over London. Canaletto, however, was obviously working later in the day than Wordsworth. The picture is widely available to look at on the web.

How did I do?

I can study mood in a classic poem. ☑

83: Dialogue in Shakespeare

In this unit you will learn
▶ to study a dialogue from Shakespeare

Get started

The following dialogue is taken from Shakespeare's *Romeo and Juliet.* Juliet's father, Capulet, is enraged because she has resisted his choice of husband. Juliet and her maidservant (the Nurse) both beg her furious father to calm down.

Juliet	Good father, I beseech you on my knees,
	Hear me with patience but to speak a word.
Capulet	Hang thee, young baggage, disobedient wretch! [thee – you]
	I tell thee what: get thee to church a' Thursday,
	Or never after look me in the face.
	Speak not, reply not, do not answer me!
	My fingers itch. Wife, we scarce thought us blest
	That God had lent us but this only child,
	But now I see this one is one too much,
	And that we have a curse in having her.
	Out on her, hilding!
Nurse	God in heaven bless her!
	You are to blame, my lord, to rate her so.
Capulet	And why, my Lady Wisdom? Hold your tongue,
	Good Prudence, smatter with your gossips, go.

Practice

Juliet is desperate that her father should listen to her. Her remarks to him at the start of the extract make this very clear.

 a What adjective does Juliet use to describe her father?

b What position does Juliet appear to be in as she pleads with her father?

c What does she ask her father to show?

Juliet's father, Capulet, does not listen to his daughter's pleadings. In fact, he suggests in the first line of his speech that she should go off and die.

2 a How does Capulet seem to be suggesting Juliet should go and kill herself?

   b Write down two (two-word) insults that Capulet then hurls at Juliet.

Capulet tells his daughter to get to church on Thursday (to be married).

3 What does he tell her never to do again if she refuses to be married?

When Capulet says *do not answer me* he is speaking as we speak today.
He also tells Juliet not to do two other things at the same time. However, he
expresses this in a variety of English that we do not use now.

4 How does Capulet tell his daughter not to *speak* or *reply* to him?

Capulet says *My fingers itch.* This is an example of where an audience (and the
director of the play) needs to make an inference from the language. In other
words, the audience needs to work out what exactly Capulet means. It seems
obvious that he does not mean he has itchy fingers.

Remember that Capulet is absolutely furious with his daughter. Think about
how he might feel and what he might want to do.

5 What do you think Capulet could mean when he says *My fingers itch*?

Capulet then goes on to address his wife who is standing watching this row. He
reminds her that in the past they had felt unlucky only to have had one child.
This was in the days when most wealthy people had as many children as they
could. Now, however, he feels differently about this single child.

6 What does Capulet now feel about having just a single child?

The Nurse tries to give Juliet some support. She says Capulet shouldn't
scold her as he is doing. Capulet insults her as he insulted Juliet. He makes
a sarcastic reference to the fact that in his view the Nurse is rather simple.

7 a What does he call the Nurse that makes a sarcastic reference to her lack
      of learning?

   b Capulet then uses an imperative phrase that effectively orders the Nurse
      to shut up. What (three-word) imperative phrase does Capulet use?

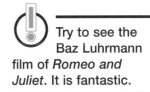
Try to see the
Baz Luhrmann
film of *Romeo and
Juliet*. It is fantastic.

How did I do?

I feel confident about studying a dialogue from Shakespeare.

84: Literary tradition

In this unit you will learn
> to study texts in the literary tradition

Get started

This passage is from the start of a story by a French writer called Guy de Maupassant.

The two cottages stood side by side at the foot of a hill not far from a small spa town. The two peasant farmers who lived in them worked very hard cultivating the poor soil to rear all the children they had. Each couple had four, and outside each house the whole gang of them played and shrieked from morning till night. The two oldest were six and the two youngest about fifteen months. Weddings and then births had occurred at more or less the same times in both houses.

The two mothers were none too sure which of the heaving brood were theirs and which were not, and both farmers were quite incapable of telling them apart. The eight names went round and round in their heads and they were forever getting them mixed up. And when one of them was wanted, the men often shouted three names before getting the right one.

They all lived on a meagre diet of soup, potatoes and fresh air. At seven in the morning, at noon, and again at six in the evening, the women called their brood in to feed them, rather as a farmer's boy might gather in the geese. The children were seated in order of age at the wooden kitchen table which shone with fifty years of wear. The mouth of the last in line scarcely came up to the top of the table. In front of them was set a bowl containing bread soaked in the water the potatoes had been boiled in, half a cabbage and three onions: and they all ate until they were full. The mother pushed food into the youngest herself. A small piece of meat in a stew on Sundays was a treat for one and all ...

Practice

The writer works very hard in the first paragraph to create a feeling of symmetry, or balance. He wants readers to have a sense of how equal the two families are.

1 a Which three-word phrase in the very first sentence suggests balance and harmony?

   b What number in the first sentence is repeated in the second sentence?

   c What do the numbers refer to in each of these two sentences?

   d How is the number four used later in the paragraph to add to the sense of symmetry?

2 a Which two adverbs used in the second sentence describe how the farmers work?

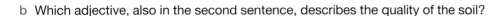

b Which adjective, also in the second sentence, describes the quality of the soil?

c Write down two verbs from the third sentence that describe the children's actions.

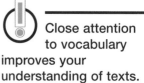 Close attention to vocabulary improves your understanding of texts.

3 Describe the lives of the two families in a sentence beginning, *Although both families ...*

4 The mothers and the fathers (the farmers) have difficulty identifying their children. Look at the second paragraph to answer these questions.

a What difference is there between the mothers and fathers in this respect?

b Why do you think this difference might exist?

c How many names go around in each farmer's head?

d What does this suggest about the way each farmer views his neighbour's children?

> The word *brood* is normally used to describe the young of animals, especially of birds. We can imagine a nest full of chicks clamouring for food.

5 a Which adjective is placed before the noun *brood* at the start of the second paragraph of the passage?

b What does the adjective suggest about the children?

> Using the word *brood* is a way of comparing the children to a family of chicks or other small animals.

6 a How is this comparison (or metaphor) continued in the third paragraph?

b What reasons may the author have for comparing the children to young animals?

Revision booster

The two families in the story are poor but happy. Writers can sum up ideas like this in **symbols**. A symbol is an object in the physical world that stands for an idea or an event. For example

A tree struck in two by lightning might be a symbol for a broken relationship.

A mask on a wall might be a symbol for disguise or deceit.

In this story, the wooden kitchen table is a symbol that sums up how poor the families are but how happy they are too.

7 a Which fact revealed in the sentence about the table suggests the families do not have spare money?

b Which single word in this sentence suggests that the table is bright and cheerful?

How did I do?

I can study texts in the literary tradition.   ☐

85: Metaphor in Shakespeare

In this unit you will learn
▶ to look at metaphor in Shakespeare

Get started

Read the following lines from Shakespeare's play, *As You Like It*. They are from the beginning of a speech made by a character called Jaques. He is reflecting on the nature of progress through life.

> All the world's a stage,
> And all the men and women merely players: [players – actors]
> They have their exits and their entrances;
> And one man in his time plays many parts,
> His acts being seven ages.

Remember that a metaphor is a comparison between different things. Metaphors can be expressed as follows.

India is a precious jewel.

The country is compared to a jewel. The comparison emphasises the preciousness and beauty of India. Sometimes metaphors can be extended.

India is a precious jewel with many faces.

The metaphor suggests that just as a cut jewel can have many sides, so India too has many different aspects.

Practice

1 a What metaphor in the extract above does Jaques use to describe the world?

b How does Jaques extend the metaphor to include living men and women?

c Jaques uses a metaphor to divide up people's lives, just as a play is divided up. What are the natural time divisions in people's lives compared to?

Read how Jaques describes the first two ages through which we live.

> At first the infant,
> Mewling and puking in the nurse's arms.
> And then the whining school-boy, with his satchel
> And shining morning face, creeping like snail
> Unwillingly to school.

Jaques suggests these first two ages are not very attractive.

2 What dominates the first of these ages?

3 a Which (single-word) verb describes the way the schoolboy walks to school?

b How is his movement made to seem slow?

4 Everything suggests that the schoolboy is miserable except for the adjective *shining*. How do you explain the fact that the schoolboy's face is shining?

Jaques then goes on to describe the third and fourth ages.

> And then the lover,
>
> Sighing like furnace, with a woeful ballad   [ballad – love song]
>
> Made to his mistress' eyebrow. Then a soldier,
>
> Full of strange oaths and bearded like the pard,   [pard – leopard]
>
> Jealous in honour, sudden and quick in quarrel,
>
> Seeking the bubble reputation
>
> Even in the cannon's mouth.

 Find a copy of this speech and read Jaques' comments about the final three ages.

5 How are the lover's sighs made to seem passionate and fiery?

6 Lovers have often been teased for praising *everything* about the person they love. How are the songs of this particular lover made to seem a bit ridiculous?

Revision booster

7 Beards were an important sign of maturity in Shakespeare's day. How is a full beard made to seem an object of worth?

8 Soldiers are concerned about their reputations *even in the cannon's mouth*. What does Shakespeare mean by this?

9 Shakespeare suggests that reputation can disappear immediately. What noun (used here as an adjective) suggests that reputation is fragile?

How did I do?

I can look at metaphor in Shakespeare.   ✔ ☐

Answers

1 All sorts of nouns

1. a *dragon*
   b *atom*
2. a *apple, star, bag, sand, finger*
   b *farmer, hand, keys, floor, hole, earth, map, mouse, nose, eyes*
3. The three common nouns are: *well, apple, day*
   The three abstract nouns are: *sorrow, revenge, idea*
4. a *book, orange, bowl, game, plans, engineers, girls, onlookers*
   b *excitement, disappointment*
   c *Jo, Saturday, Moscow*
   d *team, crowd*

2 Verbs in sentences

1. The sentences should be similar to these:
   The baby cries. Athletes run. The door slams. Friends arrive.
2. The sentences should be similar to these: *Some plants grow. These rivers flow. Their hands touch.*
3. a *some, a, the, most*
   b *people, mole, Gary, audience, monkeys*
   c *are driving, has been digging, sings, will have been listening, climb*
4. The sentences should be similar to these: *Some lions roar. The birds have been singing. The snow has been falling.*

3 Verb forms

1. *locked, brings, appears, think, smashed*
2. *to lock, to bring, to appear, to think, to smash*
3. *I go, I went, I will go; I bring, I brought, I will bring; I have, I had, I will have; I begin, I began, I will begin*
4. The modal verbs followed by the main verbs are: *will come, might help, can see, could buy, would wait*

4 Using tenses

1. a *have, uses, leave, takes, meet, am*
   b *uses, takes*
2. *My brother* is replaced by the pronoun *he*. *The walk to school* is replaced by the pronoun *it*.
3. a *I bought lemons at the market.*
   b *You were really funny.*
   c *It looked ready to rain.*
   d *His mobile irritated me.*
   e *The tiny spider spun a delicate web.*
4. *flew, looked, was, swooped, emerged*
5. *The buzzard flies to the highest peak. It looks down on the valley below. This mighty bird is indeed a fearful beast. Suddenly, it swoops down into the crevice. It emerges a few moments later with some small mammal in its beak.*

6. This sort of (simple present) account might form the commentary or voiceover for a nature programme. The simple present is often used in commentaries, most commonly for sport.

5 Infinitives

1. a *speak, speaks, spoke, am speaking/was speaking, have spoken/had spoken*
   b *fly, flies, flew, am flying/was flying, have flown/had flown*
2. *approach, feel, be, creak, grow, smash*
3. *take, cover, turn, leave, smash, roll, place, wait*
4. *Have something to eat. Take a seat. Come in and enjoy yourself.*

6 Active and passive

1. a California
   b 7.2
   c 370 miles
2. a The first sentence adds to the impression of precision by giving the exact time when the earthquake struck.
   b This sort of detailed, informative text might be found in an encyclopaedia, for example.
3. a *Three dams were destroyed.*
   b *2400 square miles were devastated.*
   c *$430 million of damage was caused.*
4. a The writer thinks it is his partner washing up.
   b Then he thinks his country is being invaded.
5. *terrible bang, unearthly explosion*
6. a his car, the telegraph wires, his neighbour's house
   b These things are too small and personal to be described in the first extract.
7. The first piece of writing provides impersonal facts that are important for recording detail and information. The second text gives us a personal and detailed account of the reaction of a human being to this disaster.

7 Using pronouns

1. *Gemma looked at the stars. They shone brightly down on her, bathing her in silvery light. She stirred as she felt the wind. It rustled through the trees. Shadows formed in the twilight. They seemed somehow kind and gentle.*
2. *That frisbee has been mine for ages but yours is just as good.*
3. *The athletes ran themselves into the ground. I am unhappy with myself. The washing up won't do itself.*
4. a *he, I, him, she, they*
   b *mine*
   c *themselves*

8 Pronouns in action

1   a   Give the bread to *him.*
    b   *She* is running towards *them.*
    c   *She* gave *it* to *her.*
2   It is planning it in it just out of it.
3   a   *you, we, us*
    b   *you* refers to the reader, *we* refers to Skipham Residents' Association, *us* refers to everybody local who is affected by the plans.
4   a   *ladder, roundabout, banana*
    b   *red, broken, overripe*
5   The phrases should be similar to these:
    a   *the old painting in the gallery near the station*
    b   *the warm sunshine on the people at the beach*

9 Prepositions in phrases

1   The alterations should be similar to these: *The dog was* **on/beside** *the table. Thomas played* **in/with** *the sand. She arrived well* **after** *the start of the concert.*
2   a   *its sinister grin*
    b   *boat, water*
3   a   *The girl in the red coat, the gates of the city, worm holes in space, Men in Black, a film with a message, A rat without a tail, the legs of the chair*
    b   *in, through, of, in, in, with, without, between, of*
4   *The fish in the pond, The ship with the sail, A knife without a proper blade, The secret cupboard behind the wall, Alice in Wonderland, The broken glass on the dirty pavement, Clouds above the Earth, Caves inside the mountain, The ground beneath your feet, The cat on the seat beside you*
5   *The cat* **on** *the seat* **beside** *you*

10 Linking clauses

1   *he stopped suddenly, it was too late, the passengers disembarked, the aircraft refuelled*
2   All the clauses are linked with commas.
3   *He moved towards us. It was dark. I was scared.*
4   *before, when, while*
5   *Before I left, I thought hard about it. When they've had enough, they'll leave. While it continues, it's a real problem.*

11 Using connectives

1   a   *Arun, Harry, I*
    b   *think, made, flies, have, collect*
    c   *tea, planes, fun, fossils*
2   The sentences should be similar to these: *Sid cooks dinner unless his mum does it for him. He makes the toast while his eggs are boiling. He washes up because nobody else will do it for him. He cleans his teeth as/while he watches the television.*
3   a   *Having waved to the crowds, the president returned to his office. Having beaten the egg, he poured it into the mixer. Having spoken to the press, Kirsty went back to her hotel.*
    b   *After waving to the crowds, the president returned to his office. After beating the egg, he poured it into the mixer. After speaking to the press, Kirsty went back to her hotel.*

12 Combining clauses

1   *howled, drove, has snowed, was, have finished, agreed*
2   a   *whenever*
    b   *or*
    c   *but*
    d   *before*
3   a   *Feeling miserable, Andre walked home. /Walking home, Andre felt miserable.*
    b   *Laughing at her own joke, the tears rolled down her cheeks./The tears rolling down her cheeks, she laughed at her own joke.*
    c   *Soaring nearly 9000 metres into the sky, Everest is the world's highest mountain.*
4   a   *Completed last year, the centre has been a success.*
    b   *Cooked in butter, these mushrooms are delicious.*
    c   *Encrusted with rubies, this is a beautiful necklace.*
5   *The centre, completed last year, has been a success. These mushrooms, cooked in butter, are delicious.*

13 Phrases and clauses

1   a   *phrase*
    b   *clause*
    c   *phrase*
    d   *clause*
    e   *phrase*
    f   *clause*
2   a   *she*
    b   *accidents*
    c   *the angry elephant*
3   *some people at the stall*
4   a   *The old lady was a happy person who made friends easily.*
    b   *It is a big problem which/that causes lots of disagreements.*
    c   *Think about these people whose lives have been changed.*
5   *The alien was a thoughtful being who always helped others. The alien, who was a thoughtful being, always helped others.*

14 Using adjectives

1 *wonderful, great, brilliant, funny, warm*
2 *Some overripe grapes, An aggressive hooligan, My painful bruise, The shattered glass, A painted clown, Your barking dog*
3 The noun phrases should be similar to these: *a deadly snake, the patient fisherman, some tall trees, a green Martian, the roaring fire, those dark caves*
4 Answers will vary, but all should be adjectives.
5 The adjectives chosen will vary, but the rewritten passage should be similar to this: *The furious doctor slammed the door. He strode towards me and pushed his angry face into mine. I could see his dark eyes level with my own. I noticed on his white jacket a streak of blood.*

15 Using adverbs

1 Possible answers are: *shouted noisily/loudly, ate hungrily/greedily, scribbled messily/hurriedly*
2 The sentences should be similar to: *I nearly cried. I ran well. I am thinking now. I never skateboard. I flew there.*
3 The sentences should be similar to:
   a *Her clothes are never/always/often tidily folded.*
   b *Astoundingly, we managed to win a game. Sadly, the swimming pool will be forced to close. Hopefully, we can go on holiday this year.*
4 *excellently, almost, frequently, just, now*

16 Verbs and adverbs

1 *Glanced* suggests she looked at it quickly. *Examined* suggests she studied it hard.
2 The sentences should be similar to this: Adelina *strode/marched/limped/hobbled/skipped/ran* to the door.
3 This answer will depend on the verbs chosen.
4 The sentences should be similar to these: The dragon *soared/fluttered...*, Ewan *munched/gulped/swallowed/wolfed/nibbled...*, The army was *defeated/destroyed/decimated.*
5 The sentences should be similar to this: Adelina walked *happily/noisily/clumsily/delicately/slowly....*
6 The answers should be similar to this: The king *rode gallantly* into battle with his knights. He *struck* his rival with a battleaxe. His enemy *fell heavily* to the ground. Arrows *flew dangerously* past the king's ears. He *cried* to his soldiers, 'Enough! No more!' The king and his warriors *returned victoriously* to their castle.

17 Spelling and sounds

1 The vowel sounds are short, long, long, short, short, short.
2 *f* with your upper teeth and your lower lip. *g* with the back of your tongue and the roof of your mouth. *m* with your lips. *t* with the front of your tongue and the roof of your mouth.
3 The rules followed are
   d a c a b a b c d c
4 *freest, greatest, fittest, maddest, tiniest, barest, reddest, angriest*

18 Spelling homophones

1 *flower, waste, threw, night, write, peace*
2 a *place* or *situation*
   b *here*
3 *They're driving over now. Here comes the bus. He doesn't know where it is. They like their new house. I can't hear you very well. They're not doing it properly. Did he wear a tie? Sit over there. There's a problem. The problem is theirs.*
4 All the uses of *its/it's* are incorrect.

19 Spelling errors (1)

1 a *have*
   b *of*
   c *have*
2 a *our, are*
   b *are, our*
   c *our, are*
3 *have, our, a lot, in fact, our, have, in fact, our, have, have*

20 Spelling errors (2)

1 a *quiet*
   b *quiet*
   c *quietly*
   d *quite*
   e *quite*
2 *practises, almost, although, quiet, advice, already, quite, all ready, almost, although*

21 Vowel length

1 Examples of long *a* are: *main, say, rate, weight.*
2 Examples of long *e* are: *weed, read, brief.*
   Examples of long *i* are: *might, why, slide.*
3 Examples of long *o* are: *slow, cone, groan.*
   Examples of long *u* are: *grew, flute, mood.*
4 Short *a*: calendar, catalogue, carrot.
   Short *e*: incensed, centre, reception.
   Short *i*: acid, cinema, city.
   Short *o*: economy, costly, cotton.
   Short *u*: custard, company, current.
   Long *a*: case, cable, decay.
   Long *e*: receive, deceit, ceiling.
   Long *i*: recite, incite, excitable.

Long *o*: coast, raincoat, honeycomb.
Long *u*: accumulate, accuse, incurable.

5 a A soft *c* is created by short and long *e* and *i* vowel sounds.

  b After a soft *c*, the long *e* vowel sound is spelled *ei*.

6 Adding the suffixes makes: *greener, greenest, holder, holding, spinner, spinning, sooner, soonest, gunner, gunning, gunned, dreading, dreaded.*

22 Spelling suffixes

1 *hopeful, sorrowful, beautiful, painful, successful*

2 The *y* changes to an *i*.

3 It turns it into an adjective.

4 a *hopefully, sorrowfully, beautifully, painfully, successfully*

  b The suffix *ly* turns adjectives into adverbs.

5 a *picked, raced, dried, obliged, applied; picking, racing, drying, obliging, applying*

  b The *e* is dropped (so that there's only one of them).

  c The *y* changes to an *i*.

6 a *value, dispose*

  b The final *e* of the stem has been dropped.

7 *possible, breakable, lovable, horrible, respectable, sliceable*

23 Making plurals

1 *fires, matches, messes, missions, boxes, plantations, flashes, televisions*

2 *pansies, lives, plays, caddies, cliffs, leaves, ospreys, reefs*

3 *The men looked after the geese. His teeth came out in the potatoes. The women played with the yo-yos. The tomatoes outlasted the mangoes. The mice went to the discos.*

4 The answers should be similar to these: *cubes of sugar, cups of coffee, glasses of milk, pats of butter, grains of sand*

24 Writing speech

1 *The doctor went back to her surgery.
"Where have you been?" asked her secretary.
"I went to the chemist to get some pills," replied the doctor. "I have a bad headache."
She took off her coat and walked into her office.*

2 *"Stop!" he shouted. "I want to get off."
"What's the problem?" she asked.
"It's a good painting," said Maisie. "Why don't you hang it on the wall?"*

3 The passage should be similar to this: *The doctor went back to her surgery. Her secretary asked her where she had been. The doctor replied that she had gone to the chemist to get some pills because she had a bad headache. She took off her coat and walked into her office.*

25 Punctuating speech

1 a *"Do you like apples?" asked Maddox. "They're my favourite fruit."*

  b *Amber shouted, "Stop!"*

  c *"Is it muddy?" asked the trooper.*

  d *"Go!" shouted the excited driver behind me. "What are you waiting for?"*

  e *"My cousin is coming tonight," he replied.*

2 *Amelia and Ollie walked quickly to the edge of the cliff.
"Is this where it happened?" asked Ollie.
"I don't know," replied Amelia. "But I think it was somewhere round here."
The two of them walked briskly on.*

26 Commas in action

1 a *This is the warmest, sunniest, driest summer on record.*

  b *The suppliers sent apples, bananas, pears, grapes, mangoes and oranges.*

2 a *Ashley groaned, "My feet are aching."*

  b *"Take him away," said the spiteful prince.*

3 a *The Sears Tower, once the world's tallest building, dominates Chicago.*

  b *Dogs, our best friends, evolved from wolves.*

  c *Jenna, my cousin, is a farmer.*

4 There are many different answers to this, though it is important to avoid overusing the connective *and*.

  a *I don't want to go to the post office because/as there's always a queue.*

  b *I was working on the computer when the virus struck.*

  c *I listened to the noise from next door and it deafened me.*

  d *The rabbit leapt from the hat while the magician smiled.*

  e *Bananas are my favourite fruit but/though I've never liked apples.*

  f *I couldn't do it though I tried very hard.*

27 Using apostrophes

1 *the tiger's roar, the flower's scent, the witch's broom*

2 *the parrots' shrieking, the jewels' value, the boxes' destination*

3 a *he's driving*

  b *they're laughing*

  c *I don't like it*

  d *we shouldn't*

  e *they mustn't*

4 a *The casino finally closed its doors.*

  b *It's been a wonderful place.*

  c *I think it's tremendous the way it's always been open.*

  d *Its problem was a lack of customers.*

28 Foregrounds in sentences

1 *In a second, he'll be coming. In a fury, she strode off. On a lonely hilltop, he lay down silently.*

2 The sentences should be similar to these: *Unhappily, they parted for the last time. Eagerly, the children ran into the fairground.*

3 *If you don't stop messing around, I'm going to lose my temper. When she found out, it was a real problem. Until the next time, take care.*

4 *Laughing all the time, he watched the film. Crying loudly, the baby woke me. Breathing deeply, she prepared her performance.*

5 The foregrounded features (in sentence order) are: a participle phrase, an adverb, an adverbial phrase

29 Sentence expansion

1 The sentences should be similar to these: *She walks to the park. I read magazines. The cat plays with the mouse.*

2 The sentences should be similar to these: *Stephan drives a car. I have money. The baker makes bread.*

3 The extensions should be similar to these: *She walks to the park in the town. I always read magazines. The white cat plays with the grey mouse.*

4 The extensions should be similar to these: *Stephan drives a car with a dent. I have money in my pocket. The baker makes bread by hand.*

5 The extensions with connectives should be similar to these: *She walks to the park and I drive to the shops. I read magazines while I'm in the car. The cat plays with the mouse and then she kills it. Stephan drives a car so he can get to work on time. I have money but I don't have any sense. The baker makes bread until he has enough to sell.*

30 Synonyms for effect

1 three times

2 The passage could be written in the following way. *Think* only had to be replaced in two instances. *I believe that all passengers on coaches should be made to wear seatbelts. I feel that many lives would be saved if this were to happen. I consider it very important that this suggestion should become law.*

3 There are many possible synonyms for these words. These are the more common ones.
   a *chat, converse, discuss*
   b *speak, confer, consult*
   c *yell, screech, roar*

4 *spoke, walked, walked, removed, put, walked*

5 See 8 below.

6 *was speaking*

7 See 8 below.

8 With the verb replaced, the new passage should be similar to this. It will not, of course, be identical.
Dawkins bellowed furiously at his team mates and then marched away. He strode into the changing room, ripped off his boots and threw them angrily on the floor. He was muttering quietly to himself when Forsyth noisily barged in.

31 Paragraphs

1 As reptiles: *Crocodiles are cold blooded and can stay still for a very long time. They do not have live young like mammals but lay eggs.*
In captivity: *There's an extremely large crocodile at Paignton Zoo. Some people keep them as pets.*
Worldwide: *Crocodiles are native to many countries including Australia. Lots of crocodiles live in African rivers.*
As predators: *Crocodiles are predators, which means they hunt live prey. They drag their victims under water and kill them not with their teeth but by drowning.*
To look at: *They are mainly a sort of light green in colour. Their eyes are near the tops of their heads.*

2 Crocodiles are mainly light green. Sometimes they are browny grey for camouflage. Their skins are knobbly and rough. They have sharp teeth. Their legs are short, squat and powerful. Their eyes are near the top of their heads.

3 *... they can blend in with the muddy rivers and vegetation ...*
... they have rows of teeth as sharp as razors.
... they can see above the water without revealing their bodies.

32 Language analysis

1 The pronoun is *we* and the rats have taken seven of them.

2 a *We love the forest.*
   b The sentences should be similar to these: *I play the piano. They steal the words.*

3 a *really*
   b This sentence is a repetition of the idea in the opening sentence and it ends with an exclamation mark to express the strength of the emotion. It is also a very short sentence and this too adds emphasis.

4 *splendid, sprout, soil*

5 *sprout, tower, swish*

6 *Who could feel anything but joy to see such a beautiful place?*

7 *We dance and we play* and *the leaves swish above*

8 The connective is *as* and the second clause is *we run through the woods.*

9 *splendid, green, mighty, old, beautiful*
10 *free, lucky*

33 Grammatical features

1 a Jamal has gone to the surgery for a blood test.
 b He is quite pleased because he is missing school.
 c Jamal's mother seems not to share this view.
2 *Miss school this morning.*
 Arrive at the surgery.
3 Jamal uses the present tense.
4 a Jamal feels his dignity is under threat because everyone in the surgery knows he is having trouble going to the toilet.
 b *stride*
 c He walks in this way to show the rest of the waiting room that he is confident and relaxed.
5 He makes his new sentence stronger by repeating the word *very* before the phrase *bad news.*
6 These sentences could be completed in many different ways. The original statement in the first sentence must be made stronger by what follows.
 I don't like oysters. Actually, I really, really hate them.
 It was funny. Actually, it was hilarious.
 I don't seem to remember it. Actually, I've completely forgotten it.

34 Retrieving information

1 a Most of the Earth is covered in water.
 b The highest mountain is around 9000 metres.
 c The fertile and temperate regions are around sea level.
2 a *a moderately fertile world*
 b *a* is the determiner, *moderately* is the adverb, *fertile* is the adjective, *world* is the noun
 c *a rather strange animal*
3 *places, regions*
4 The alien describes them as *'rather large, with long necks, great teeth or extraordinarily long noses'.*
5 *mainly, generally, often, obviously*
6 *currently*
7 *rather*

35 Alphabetical texts

1 audience, believe, daughter, fierce, jealous, material, remember, separate, tomorrow, weight
2 rye, snug, so, soak, sob
3 a *Fun* must come before *funny* because the whole of *fun* is made up of letters that form only a part of *funny.*

 b *Fun* and *funny* must come before all the other words because *F* comes before *G* and *H.*
 c Happiness must come before *he* because *a* comes before *e.*
4 fun, funny, gym, gyrate, happiness, he, hear, heat, heath, heather
5 puce, pug, puggaree, pugilist, pukka, pullet, punkah, punnet, purloin, putrid

36 Presenting information

1 a The main problem with science is that it often does not seem to make sense.
 b three
2 a Her examples are separated from one another by putting them in different paragraphs.
 b These separate sentences are at the beginning and end of the text.
 c The first of these sentences introduces the idea.
3 a It doesn't seem right that the level of the water should go down.
 b She could have used the phrase *I am told.*
 c She shows the reader that she does not really understand the information. It has been explained to her by people who do understand it.
4 *My scientific friends say not. Or at least, that is what I am told.*
5 a It is obvious to the writer.
 b The obvious conclusion is not correct.
 c This supports the writer's main idea that many scientific conclusions go against common sense.
6 *Right? Another one?*
7 She may have wanted to make the text informal because science is often seen as complex and difficult. She may not have wanted to turn her readers off by using a formal style.
8 a She asks the reader to imagine being on the dinghy in the pool.
 b The reader is asked to imagine being in a discussion with the writer.
9 *Example, Question, Answer*

37 Structuring information

1 *Hercules, the name of the Roman emperor*
2 *from ancient Greek*
3 a The word *Tyrannosaurus* comes from ancient Greek.
 b It was discovered over one hundred years ago.
4 The size of a Tyrannosaurus' head is compared to a fully grown human. The height is compared to a double decker bus.

5   *Tyrannosaurus, tyrant lizard, this great dinosaur, T Rex, this extraordinary beast, a true giant, a fearful predator*

38 Reading for detail

1   a   He was discussing horses.
    b   He giggled when Jim started to talk about the Grand National.
    c   His friend whacked him on the mouth to shut him up.
    d   The prisoner seems to be from Liverpool.
    e   He was writing to someone he cared for, perhaps his partner, because he refers to the person as 'my love'.
2   a   The prisoners seem to be happy because they are chatting and laughing together. Although one of them hits Arnie, it all looks like a bit of a joke.
    b   The letter states that they are all missing home and hope to return home soon, which indicates that they are not happy at the prison.
3   Massive air attack on Liverpool coming soon.
4   No need to worry. Our soldiers are on their way to get you out of there.
5   a   The censors would probably describe Sheena's mood as depressed and miserable.
    b   She pretends that a miserable Christmas and the fact that she can't help any of her neighbours are making her sad.
    c   She pretends to blame politicians for the situation.
    d   She might be trying to make the enemy feel relaxed so that they are not prepared for surprise attacks.

39 Locating detail

1   a   at noon
    b   behind Smith Street
    c   by mid-afternoon
2   a   *officially*
    b   *gradually*
    c   *progress* (or *will progress*)
3   *The carnival begins officially; Officially, the carnival begins*
4   *at noon*
5   *in the town square, beside the library*
6   *The procession will reach the park by mid-afternoon.*
7   *will leave, will progress, will reach*
8   *begins*

40 Narrative features (1)

1   *early, during the night, already, after a while, in the end*
2   *finally*

3   The first anecdote is about the collapse of Tent 3. The second anecdote is about the teacher burning the sausages.
4   a   The first anecdote is made amusing by the way the girls use the tent as a duvet.
    b   The second anecdote is made funny because the teacher blames the cooker but everyone knows it is his fault.
5   a   *out of date*
    b   They probably believe Mr Walters cannot cook.
6   *We believed you, Mr Walters.*
7   *nobody minded at all*

41 Narrative features (2)

1   a   a tiger
    b   *incredible*
    c   The tiger bares its teeth
2   Zoe says that the enclosure was *massive* and that glass (not bars) formed a part of the boundary.
3   a   *less energetic*
    b   *lazy* or *lazier* or something similar
4   a   *After free time, On our way*
    b   Zoe puts her adverbial phrases at the start of her sentences.
5   a   *The zoo is built on a number of hills*
    b   because it doesn't matter at all now who built the zoo

42 Story structure

7   Opening: *The bedroom was full of screaming children. Wrapping paper littered the floor.* Plot development: *Niall, whose birthday it was, jumped on the bed. He started bouncing up and down.* Complication: *There was a terrible crack and the bed collapsed beneath him.* Crisis: *Niall lay in a heap of broken slats and bedclothes.* Conclusion: *'Happy Birthday,' said his mother, as she opened the door.*

43 Text structure

1   The paragraph summaries should be similar to these: *Imran describes his fear at being trapped in the cave. He relates how his hope turns to despair. He describes how hope turns to joy.*
2   a   Imran starts each paragraph with an exact record of the time.
    b   He could be suggesting that the rest of his account is accurate and true to the facts.
    c   The endings of each paragraph all mention parts of Imran's body.
    d   Ending each paragraph like this stresses Imran's physical condition to the reader.
3   a   *steady light of the torch, it's pitch black, a chink of light, the sun starts to beam through*

b   These phrases show how the steady artificial light was replaced after the accident with terrifying pitch darkness. Then, gradually, more light appears until Imran is rescued.

4   a   Sound would be important because there would be no light.

b
Quotation	Emotion
crashing like a distant storm	*horror*
blood throbbing in my ears	*isolation*
this sound of scratching	*hope*
I hear a patter	*despair*
faint music of voices	*excitement/ fear*
rocks tumbling	*joy*

5   The first point on the graph (at 10.42 on the horizontal axis) should be near the middle of the vertical axis and then the line should plummet after the rock fall. It should then move up and down according to Imran's levels of hope and despair. At the end of the account (14.34 on the horizontal axis) the line on the graph should be near the top of the vertical axis.

44 Settings in fiction

1   a ghost/horror story, a story for very young children, a science fiction novel

2   a   Waterloo is contrasted with the '*lovely Surrey lanes*'.

b   Watson comments on the contrast between '*the sweet promise of the spring*' and the two men's '*sinister quest*'.

c   Holmes seems to pay no attention to the setting at all, though the last sentence suggests he might be looking.

3   Any of these: *perfect day, bright sun, fleecy clouds, green shoots, pleasant smell, sweet promise*

4   a   *lanes, trees, hedges, shoots, earth, meadows*

b   *the heavens*

c   *spring*

d   the '*first green shoots*' coming from the trees and hedges

5   *suddenly*

45 Figurative language

1   *smiled, sat, sadly, angrily, giant, dance, play*

2   a   *The web was as delicate as the finest lace. His grating laugh was like an electric saw. The dead tree stood like a bony hand. That night, the stars shone as bright as diamonds. The wind battered the glass like an enraged giant.*

b   The dead tree and the wind

3   The first sentence is a metaphor, the second is a simile and the third is an example of personification.

46 Descriptive language

1   two

2   *It lies alone on the table unhappy at being pulled from the beach where it has lain for a million years.*

3   The first stanza is about the stone just sitting on the table looking miserable. The second stanza is about the reasons why it is so miserable.

4   *stares, glares*

5   a   *polished, bright*

b   The writer moves on to a new line when this description is over.

c   *a dark brown eye*

d   She shows she is moving on from the first part of the comparison by starting another new line.

6   a   *stares, glares*

b   The verbs are related to eyes.

c   They make the writer feel as if the stone is watching her.

7   a   *alone, unhappy*

b   *pulled*

c   It suggests the stone was taken from the beach against its will.

47 Making comparisons

1   The answers should be similar to these:

a   The acrobat is as agile as a cat.

b   Luke's shirt is as filthy as an old dishcloth.

c   The dragon's eye is like a polished ruby.

d   The alien's fingernails were like an eagle's talons.

e   The 4x4 is as ugly as a battleship.

2   The answers should be similar to these:

a   *The giant's footsteps crashed like thunder. The giant's footsteps were as loud as thunder.*

b   *Eva's eyes were like crystal. Eva's eyes were as clear as crystal.*

c   *The shark's teeth were like razors. The shark's teeth were as sharp as razors.*

3   The answers should be similar to these:

a   *T Rex was as tall as a London double decker.*

b   *Some dinosaurs could run as fast as a car.*

4   The answers should be similar to these:

a   *An octopus' tentacles are like writhing snakes. An octopus' tentacles are as sticky as limpets.*

b   *That enormous dog looks like a pony. That enormous dog is as big as a pony.*

c   *The parrot looked like a rainbow. The parrot was as colourful as a rainbow.*

48 Writing description

1   a   description

b   action

c description
d description
e action
2 a *lonely*
b *bleary*
c *sadly*
d *gloom*
e The old man is lonely and unhappy and his surroundings are miserable.
3 a *steadily*
b The adverb is used to create the impression that the rain is here to stay.
4 *slowly, painfully*
5 The old man's face is compared to a cobweb.
6 The rain on the window pane is compared to tears on unhappy cheeks.

49 Description

1 a Alex is probably writing some sort of horror story or maybe a ghost story.
b The man's eyes in the picture (they seem to follow the boy) suggest this sort of text.
2 *The beast was sleeping* or *The beast was asleep. The statue moved.*
3 a *The man's eyes seemed to follow the boy as he walked through the door.* (fourth sentence)
b *The man's eyes followed the boy as he walked through the room.*
4 *the boy, the room, a picture, the wall, a picture, a man, the boy, the door, a woman, the stairs, the boy*
5 Any number of adjectives could be chosen to add to these noun phrases. Examples are: *a faded picture, the dusty wall, an old woman, the creaking stairs*
6 The answer should be similar to these: *An old woman with grey hair, A tall woman with a sad face*

50 Creating effects

1 a *the mean wind*
b A miserable cold mood is created, as if the wind has some spiteful desire to get the man on the moor.
2 a *blew*
b *chillingly*
3 His eyes are blurred because the cold wind is making them water.
4 a He uses *st* and *k* sounds.
b A harsh and cold effect is created by these sounds.
5 The trees are compared to *naked, broken scarecrows.*
6 a This suggests the trees do not have leaves.
b *naked*

7 The most obvious way of rewriting this sentence is *And then I saw the light.* It is not as dramatic as the verbless sentence.

51 Creating mood (1)

1 a *dusty*
b They are always in the same order.
c The writer suggests that these books are never read or even moved.
2 a *a lonely spider plant; some crumpled, glossy magazines*
b *lonely, crumpled*
3 *sadly*
4 *drooped*
5 a *shiny, fantastic*
b *beaming*
c The real world of the waiting room is dusty and gloomy. This contrasts with the make-believe world which is shiny and happy.
6 *There was a lonely spider plant that drooped down sadly above them./A lonely spider plant that drooped down sadly was above them.*

52 Creating mood (2)

1 A ghost or horror story
2 a Edmund is standing on the doorstep as if building up courage to knock.
b *silently, fearfully*
3 a The house seems to be cooling the air that surrounds it.
b This makes us feel that the house is alive, with a chilly breath.
4 *silently*
5 It seems as though Edmund is being drawn into the house. Things are happening without people being there to make them happen.
6 a *silently, fearfully, suddenly, finally, silently*
b The passage makes perfectly good sense with these adverbs left out.
c The effect of leaving them out, however, is to reduce some of the feelings of suspense and tension.
7 a *gloomy light, looming shadows*
b The phrases create the sense that the interior of the house is dark and cheerless.
8 a *walked hesitantly, with cautious steps*
b They suggest that Edmund is nervous and perhaps worried about what he might find.
9 a The colour of the carpet is compared to that of dried blood.
b This might suggest accidents or murderous activities in which someone has bled. The fact the blood is dried may indicate that the horrors occurred some time ago.
10 a Unlike the rest of the extract, this sentence includes references to life and sound.

b It is placed away from the rest of the passage in a paragraph by itself.

c *far*

d The baby's distance is also emphasised by the fact that the crying is *faint.*

e The tension is increased because clearly Edmund cannot leave a crying baby alone in this house. He is going to have to continue his exploration and, like the reader, endure the fear it creates.

53 Focus in writing

2 Additional questions could be: What was the atmosphere like in the changing room? Was it easy to tie your laces or were your hands shaking? Were you disappointed to come fourth? What level do you race at? How did your body feel as you raced? What could you see and hear as you were running?

4 The second question is answered by sentence 2. The third question is answered by sentence 4. The fourth question is answered by sentence 5.

54 Conveying feelings

1 a *terrible, disorganised, chaotic*

b *A paradise on Earth*

c She likes the gentle people and their relaxed and peaceful attitude.

2 a *terrified, frightened*

b A grass snake had slithered from her lunchbox onto her lap.

c As an adult she knew these feelings were ridiculous and that made her feel foolish but she couldn't control the feeling.

3 a Erin says she likes 'the gentleness of the people'.

b Erin says she likes 'the constant clatter, rattle and hum'.

c Erin says she likes 'the vibrant, rainbow colours of the women's clothes'.

d Erin says she likes 'the exquisite local dishes, so full of flavour'.

4 a The snake is compared to a hand grasping Erin's ankle and an evil climbing plant.

b She can't scream and she is paralysed.

c Erin puts 'aggression' in inverted commas because she wants to show that this is only the way *other* people or animals might view her actions. She and her readers know that her 'aggression' was, in reality, an accident.

d After the incident, Erin's fear of snakes disappears for ever.

5 *In my opinion it's a paradise ...*

... in my view, just the constant clatter ...

To my way of thinking they were the creatures ...

My own feeling about this strange episode ...

55 Character in fiction (1)

1 *kind/kindest, gentle*

2 a The sentence should be similar to: *Sammy Sneak looks extremely odd, like a pantomime villain.*

b Sammy is delighted with his appearance.

c His feelings about his appearance suggest he is vain, and doesn't see himself as others see him.

d Sammy is creeping around, snooping and spying on other people.

3 a It is a warm, friendly, *cuddly* sort of place.

b The reader can confidently infer that Sammy is a *sneak*.

4 a The children are excited and looking forward to building their tree house.

b Data is into technology. This can be inferred from his name and from the fact that he wants to take his laptop up to the tree house.

c Sammy's plans are likely to involve destroying the tree house in one way or another.

56 Character in fiction (2)

1 a *slipped quietly*

b These actions could suggest many different things about the person: the person could be a thief, a prisoner, or a child in trouble, for example.

2 a *tenderly*

b Jonah is cooling his brother's forehead with a wet flannel.

c He slips through the door so as not to wake his brother.

3 In the answer to 2c there was much more information to go on. Therefore a much more informed assessment of Jonah's character was possible.

4 *trembling*

5 a *balloon face*

b *narrowed eyes*

c *uneven yellow teeth*

6 His mouth, his nose and his tongue are also described.

7 The narrator is covered in flecks of spit.

8 There are many possible answers. The answer should be similar to this: *Humbert was an aggressive and unpleasant man.*

57 Creating character

1 Maxi is short, he looks strong, he has blue eyes, he has a chipped tooth.

7 The reader doesn't know at first that Maxi is a cruel man. The second description confirms that he is nasty and powerful.

58 Assessing character

1 a 750 miles in five days
  b Abigail may have put these numbers at the start of her account to emphasise straight away the difficulty of what she did.
  c According to her, the most painful part of long-distance cycling is the saddle sore.
  d The words *agonising* and *blinding* are used to emphasise this pain.
  e Abigail describes car drivers as *thoughtless*.
2 a Abigail does not blame other people when she knows something is her own fault.
  b The accident knocks out one of her teeth and breaks her nose.
  c Her response to the accident indicates she is tough and strong and can ignore pain.
  d The last part of the last sentence emphasises the three things needed to be an endurance athlete.
3 a Abigail used to think that endurance events were for 'freaks' but now she realises they provide 'enormous challenges'.
  b The gift that sparked this change in attitude was a new bike.
  c She came to see her bike as a 'friend' and a 'partner'.
4 Abigail gets very impatient with Evelyn when she starts to slow down and then she speaks quite aggressively to her when she finally stops. Afterwards, Abigail realises she was hard but she thinks she did the right thing. This all shows that Abigail puts herself and her achievements above other people and their feelings. She gets frustrated when others threaten to get in the way of her success.

59 Speech in literature

1 a *creepy*
  b *little girl*
2 a *he replied*
  b You would find this structure in books for very young children, perhaps fairy stories.
  c *said he*
3 *shake*
4 It suggests the woman is trapped (behind bars) and wants to escape.
5 The narrator gets out of bed to feel the wallpaper.
6 She tries to avoid waking John up.
7 She eats properly only when John is there.
8 She was about to say something like *but not better in mind*.
9 a He is talking about his wife as if she is not there.
  b It is normal if people are not there. It is also normal if the person being talked about is a baby.

60 Formal and informal (1)

1 a *Hi guys*
  b exclamation mark
  c *whooeee*
2 *Sorry not to have been in touch for so long.*
3 a *I'm, here's*
  b *I am, here is*
4 *next, now*
5 *Press down firmly with both hands. Next, push the rockers into place.*

61 Formal and informal (2)

1 a Chloe-Louise's audience is her friends.
  b Her purpose is to invite them to a party.
  c Her invitation is far too formal and unfriendly for her audience and her purpose.
2 a *Hi* is a much more friendly and informal way of starting a letter.
  b They probably refer to the SeaSpray Centre by name because it makes it sound like an exciting and fun place to be, and to make it absolutely clear where the party is taking place.
  c At the end of the first letter, it seems as if Chloe-Louise thinks of her guests as a bit of a nuisance.
  d The ending of the second letter makes it seem as though Chloe-Louise actually likes her guests and wants them to come to her party.
3 *Tell me as soon as you can.*
4 *Can you make it?*
5 *I look forward to seeing you there!*
6 a The swimming pool has wave machines, a 60-metre slide and the Devil's Rapids.
  b There's an Old Ranch barbecue serving Smoky Joe Burgers.

62 Instructions and advice

1 The sentences should be similar to these: *Drive home safely. Stay on the pavement. Put your coat on if it rains.*
2 The sentences should be similar to these: *Don't take drugs. Don't waste water. Don't go out of sight.*
3 a *turn, run, plunge*
  b *Do not put off doing this.*
4 *you*
5 *Come with me/Think about coming with me. Take a chance/Consider taking a chance.*
6 *could forget, might find, may want*

63 Informative style

1 This type of informative text is most likely to be found in an encyclopedia.
2 RMS Titanic, *the world's most celebrated passenger ship, She, a vast and impressive*

colossus, the largest and most sumptuous liner in the world, This great ship, Titanic, Titanic

3 The writer conveys the impression of an extraordinary and magnificent ship.

4 a *Titanic* was nearly 300 metres in length and could hold over 3500 people.

   b *Titanic* had swimming pools, saunas and squash courts.

5 *each propeller was as large as a tennis court*

6 *completed, thought*

64 Writing complaints

1 a *You claim.*

   b *I suggest.*

2 a The hotel made the claim that it maintained '*the highest standards of quality and service*'.

   b This sort of claim is often made in advertisements.

3 The car park was too small, the check-in was unattended and the room was without soap or towels.

4 a *tiny.* If the hotel had provided a bigger car park then the writer wouldn't have had the difficult walk.

   b *public*

5 a *We were forced to park half a mile away on a public road.*

   b She expresses it like this because it would sound ridiculous to blame something on a car park.

6 a *haul*

   b She means to emphasise how heavy the cases were. If the car park had been bigger then she wouldn't have had to carry the cases all that way.

7 The writer says her daughter was in the shower before she noticed there was no soap or towels. This was obviously inconvenient.

65 Language of advice

1 *Everyone*

2 *You*

3 *We*

4 *They*

5 a *should*

   b *eat, reduce*

6 *Read on, and all will become clear.*

7 a *packed*

   b soup

   c sea water

8 a The point about to be strengthened is that ready meals are packed with salt.

   b The writer provides an example to strengthen the point.

66 Explanations

1 a at junior school

   b the Saxons and the Romans

   c epidemics, witch hunts and famines

2 a *love, were* (*were* is a past tense form of the verb *be*)

   b The first verb is in the (simple) present tense and the second is in the (simple) past.

   c In the first sentence, the writer is describing the way she feels now. In the second sentence, she is explaining the way people were in the past.

3 a She says there are no women teachers and that history is full of men.

   b *the first reason, the second reason*

   c Some of her friends

   d *definitely*

4 *The second reason is more important, though.*

5 *Think about it.*

6 She calls historical men *superheroes* and she uses an exclamation mark too.

67 Reports

1 a the pump room

   b at the end of the year

   c the early 1980s

2 a *Considering its age*

   b *Refurbished last in the early 1980s*

3 a The pool linings have been replaced.

   b *just*

   c The action is expressed in the present perfect tense.

   d *will*

4 *the pump room will be refitted, these areas must be given attention*

5 *re*

6 must

68 Promotional writing

1 a at the head of the Thames estuary

   b during the middle of the Victorian era

   c the buildings

2 a *sits*

   b *proudly*

3 a Shoebury is described as being at the *head* of the estuary.

   b This metaphor was probably chosen to suggest a position at the very top of things.

4 a *She*

   b It makes Shoebury seem more like a living, breathing person.

   c Ships are sometimes referred to by the same pronoun.

5 a *a crucial role*

   b *a mighty garrison*

   c *their superb buildings*

6 a *She has welcomed visitors to these islands for centuries.*

   b *The town has had a crucial role in our defence against invaders in more recent* times. *A mighty garrison was settled during the middle of the Victorian era.*

7   a   *for centuries*
      b   *during the middle of the Victorian era*

69 Structuring an argument

1   The sentence should be similar to this: *Kids who tag walls are artists, they are angry and they are part of the tradition of cave painting.*

2   *However, I can't agree with any of this. I can't, however, agree with any of this. I can't agree, however, with any of this.*

3   a   *To my mind*
      b   The sentence should be similar to this: *In my view, smoking should be banned in public places.* Note that the initial phrase should be separated from the rest of the sentence with a comma.

4   *Some people, Others, A minority*

5   a   *artists, taggers, tag bandits, tag mites, bored attention seekers*
      b   The references suggest that she doesn't have a very high opinion of these kids. She thinks of them as irritating little nuisances.

70 Persuasive techniques (1)

1   a   *you*
      b   It makes the reader feel singled out. It is as if the writer is talking directly to the reader.

2   a   There are three rhetorical questions in this extract.
      b   Most people would wish to answer these questions with a *yes*.
      c   The writer hopes this will have the effect of making readers answer *yes* to the final question as well.

3   a   Helpers are made to feel that they will not be giving up *too* much of their own time.
      b   The second phrase shows that the writer understands time is valuable to people. It is as if people own the time that they are donating to the fair.
      c   The third phrase shows that the effort made by volunteers is for something worthwhile.

4   *enthusiastic, energetic*

5   a   *we are looking for*
      b   *We need*
      c   *help*

6   a   *our*
      b   It suggests that the writer feels proud of it. It is something that belongs to the writer but which the writer clearly wants to share.

71 Persuasive techniques (2)

1   a   *friendly, lovely*
      b   *abused*

c   The word *litter* is emphasised by putting it at the end of the passage, giving it a sentence all to itself and completing it with an exclamation mark.

2   a   *The visitor's name? Litter!*
      b   Possible answers are: *Graffiti! There aren't enough teachers. Punish the owners!*

4   a   The town is personified by calling it *friendly*.
      b   Litter is personified by calling it *a visitor.*

5   This makes it seem as if a happy person is being made sad by an unwelcome guest (like at a party) barging in and spoiling everything.

6   a   *lout, hooligan, yob*
      b   Cara hates litter – she thinks it is as destructive as the kind of unpleasant people she describes.
      c   She hopes her rhetorical question will encourage other people to join her in the fight against litter.

7   a   five
      b   She includes a variety of things to give different sorts of people the chance to contribute in their own way.
      c   She repeats the word *please* three times.
      d   Cara makes it seem as though dropping litter is like being nasty to a close friend.

72 Persuasion

1   a   The audience for this letter is the local community.
      b   The writer tries to get the audience on his side by calling them his friends.

2   a   *close*
      b   *our local sports centre*
      c   *disaster*

3   a   The main idea of this sentence is that everyone uses the sports centre.
      b   Mothers, children, the elderly and students

4   The writer argues that: people will become overweight and unfit; teenagers will have nothing to do; many people will be thrown out of work.

5   a   *It will be devastating.*
      b   The effect of repeating these similar phrases is to stress the point that the closure of the centre would be a very bad thing.

6   a   The word is *all*. Obviously not everyone will become unfit if the centre closes.
      b   *thrown out of work*

7   a   *We have been asked to play.*
      b   *I was taken to hospital.*
      c   *We have been beaten.*
      d   *I was knocked on the head.*

73 Journalism

1   a   *The Echo can today reveal, The Echo is also able to disclose*
      b   *reveal, disclose*

2 *well-placed sources*
3 a The verb *reveal* is meant to suggest that the councillors have something to hide.
   b *luxury*
   c It is meant to suggest that the councillors are having an excellent time at the expense of the local taxpayers.
4 a *'fact finding'*
   b The councillors (or the council)
   c Readers are meant to think that the statement is not true. They are supposed to think the council is deceiving them.

74 Biography

1 a the rain
   b *flood*
2 a *smiling from ear to ear*
   b The reader immediately gets the impression that he is a friendly, welcoming sort of character.
3 a The first and the second paragraphs both refer to rain.
   b The second paragraph moves the subject matter on by referring to the rain in Malaya.
4 This detail suggests that perhaps William Brown is living a little in the past. Maybe he is unwilling to move along with the times.
5 a cricket
   b It suggests he was living a traditional life, playing traditional colonial games.
6 a *is raining, is smiling*
   b *arrive, knock, welcomes*
7 a *have had, have done*
   b *had lived, had improved*
   c *was playing, was staying*

75 Viewpoint in non-fiction

1 a *heavenly, worshipful*
   b *rocky, rugged*
   c *sculpted god*
2 a Jared probably feels that climbing a mountain like this is like going on a visit to paradise.
   b People often kneel when they are praying. Perhaps Jared feels as if he is paying this sort of respect to the mountain.
3 a *embrace*
   b It suggests that Jared's feelings towards the mountain are similar to those he would have for someone he loved.
4 a He suspects her of littering the camp site, knocking heads off flowers and swearing.
   b It indicates that he cares deeply about his environment.
5 *this sacred mountain, a devil in paradise*
6 a The reader might feel more sympathy with Alanis due to her inexperience.

b The reader might now feel that Jared could have given Alanis advice, rather than losing his temper with her.

76 Point of view (1)

1 a *children of the well to do, wealthy children, The rich kids, spoilt brats, unbearably spoilt brats*
   b The chain suggests that the author dislikes the children she describes very much.
   c It seems Penny Boynton is being a little unfair. She is judging all the children in exactly the same way. They surely cannot *all* have been that bad!
2 The verbs suggest that the children are not doing anything at all very serious. Boynton is indicating that the children are wasting their time on unimportant things.
3 *In their early days*
4 a *They catered only for children of the well to do in their early days.*
   b She avoided starting both the second and the third sentence with the word *They*. It would have been a little clumsy to have done this.
5 *now*
6 a *Stage schools, They, centres of excellence, They*
   b She now describes them as wonderful.
7 The adjectives are: *constructive, stimulating, excellent*
8 The determiners (*all* and *every*) suggest that now *all* children can benefit from stage school, not just the privileged few.

77 Point of view (2)

1 The writer feels that the campaign was unimpressive and very disappointing.
2 a *When you've finished chattering, I'll be able to speak.*
   b *After all that, it was absolutely no good.*
3 She wants readers to notice this phrase because she thinks a lot of time was wasted before the World Cup which *in the end* was not worthwhile.
4 The sentences should be similar to these:
   a *After all those miles of newsprint there was nothing worth reading.*
   b *After the endless discussions about tactics and formations we still couldn't play.*
5 The writer is suggesting that since everyone knows about the failure of the England team it does not need to be spelled out. She suggests that everyone knows what a waste of time the whole thing was.
6 a The phrase indicates the enormous amount of newspaper space taken up with the World Cup.
   b *endless*

c She seems to think talk about tactics is rather a waste of time.

d According to the writer, the footballers made boasts and promises.

7 a *defend*

b She would probably have preferred England to have lost playing more attacking football.

8 a It suggests that fans saw the defeat as something terrible and disastrous.

b The question mark suggests that the writer is prepared to ask whether the defeat really was so bad.

c The writer seems to think that it is not the end of the world because too much fuss was made about it in the first place.

78 Purpose and viewpoint

1 a *pearl*

b *small, friendly, interesting, exciting*

c The word *rainbow* suggests variety and colour.

2 a The writer tries to create the impression that there is lots to do in Bahrain and that it is very welcoming.

b The purpose of the writing is to try to persuade people to visit the island.

3 Contrasts between new and old include those between planes and boats, shopping malls and souks/street markets, and five star cuisine compared to food off street stalls.

4 a *fine hotels, luxurious shopping malls*

b *boasts*

5 a *busy, bustling*

b The writer is suggesting that the streets are popular with shoppers.

6 *the more adventurous*

7 a Jabal Dukhan, the burial mounds or the beach

b *admire, marvel, relax*

8 The whole paragraph picks up on the rainbow idea by actually describing the variety of colourful things that visitors can do.

9 These words make it seem as though visitors are being personally welcomed by the writer.

10 The end of the first paragraph encourages us to visit. The start of the second paragraph tells us what will happen when we do visit.

11 The writer hopes that repeating the invitation will actually encourage the reader to come to Bahrain.

79 Fact and opinion

1 a The Open Day will be on Tuesday, 6th April and will start at 9.30.

b The Open Day will start off in Room P4.

2 Tim believes people will have an *excellent* day.

3 A modal verb is used in this way in the first sentence.

4 *exhibitions of students' work, demonstrations of activities, chances for parents, a variety of events, introduction from Mrs Cooke*

5 a *We do hope you will be able to attend.*

b He is trying to make his audience feel as welcome as possible. He is trying to encourage as many people to come as he can.

6 *It's going to be an excellent day.*

80 Shakespeare's language

1 *This royal throne of kings, This earth of majesty*

2 *this seat of Mars, This other Eden*

3 a *fortress*

b *a wall, a moat*

4 *Envy* would cause other countries to attack England.

5 The pronoun is *herself*.

6 *the hand of war*

7 *This precious stone*

8 John of Gaunt thinks that England is a precious, wonderful paradise. It is blessed with natural defences that make it safe from envious outsiders.

9 *This* creates the impression of England being here and now. Something that John of Gaunt is a part of and can almost touch. *That* would make England seem more distant and less close to John of Gaunt.

10 There are about twelve, depending on how you count. You could have any of the following: *This royal throne of kings, this sceptred isle, This earth of majesty, this seat of Mars, This other Eden, This fortress built by nature, this little world, This precious stone, This blessed plot, this Earth, this realm, this England*

81 Speech in Shakespeare

1 a An Egyptian charmer gave Othello's mother the handkerchief.

b Othello's mother gave him the handkerchief when she was dying.

c She told him to give the handkerchief to his wife when he married.

2 a The clairvoyant could almost read people's thoughts.

b The handkerchief would make Othello's mother appear desirable. The word in the text, *amiable*, now means just good natured and friendly. Its meaning has changed since Shakespeare's time.

c His spirits would hunt after 'new fancies'. In other words, he would look for other women.

3 He asks Desdemona to make the handkerchief her darling.

4 a Othello's father's eye is referred to first.

b His father's eye would hold his mother 'loathly'.

c He uses the adjective 'precious'.

d He believes they will all go to hell.

5 Othello seems extremely superstitious. He makes a lot of the omens and predictions surrounding the handkerchief and what might happen if it were lost. He is being very hard on Desdemona as well. After all, she didn't intend to lose his handkerchief.

6 *An Egyptian gave that handkerchief to my mother.*

7 Nowadays the word is used to describe someone who is charming (perhaps even falsely charming).

8 Othello describes the action of getting married (to a wife).

9 *loathe*

10 *It would, on it*

82 Classic verse

1 a *Earth has not anything to show more fair;*

b *dull*

2 *majesty*

3 *the beauty of the morning*

4 a Three of the following: *ships, towers, domes, theatres, temples.*

b Everything is silent because it is early in the morning.

5 The buildings go right up to the edge of the fields. The air is *smokeless.* Everything is very clean.

6 *valley, rock, hill*

7 a *In his first splendour*

b *splendour*

c *his*

8 a *his*

b The houses seem to be sleeping.

c a *mighty heart*

9 *calm*

83 Dialogue in Shakespeare

1 a *good*

b She appears to be on her knees.

c *patience*

2 a Capulet suggests that Juliet should go and hang herself.

b *young baggage, disobedient wretch*

3 If she refuses to get married, Capulet tells his daughter never to look him in the face again.

4 *Speak not, reply not.*

5 Capulet probably means that his fingers itch to thump his daughter. He is trying to control his urge to hit her. His fingers seem to have a life of their own that he can't control.

6 Capulet says that one child is one too many.

7 a *Lady Wisdom*

b *Hold your tongue*

84 Literary tradition

1 a *side by side*

b *two*

c In the first sentence the number refers to the cottages, in the second it refers to the farmers.

d Both families have four children each.

2 a *very hard*

b *poor*

c *played, shrieked*

3 The answer should be similar to this: *Although both families are very poor and work hard, they seem to live happy lives.*

4 a The fathers have even more difficulty remembering their children's names than the mothers.

b This could be because the farmers are away from their children in the fields all day.

c Eight names go around in each farmer's head.

d It suggests that each farmer sees his neighbour's children as his own.

5 a *heaving*

b It suggests the children are in constant movement.

6 a The word *brood* is repeated. Their mothers are described like farmers' boys calling in the geese.

b The author may have compared the children to young animals because they are as wild and as unruly as animals. It is also a good comparison because the story is about a farm.

7 a The table is fifty years old. The families cannot afford to buy new things.

b *shone*

85 Metaphor in Shakespeare

1 a Jaques compares the world to a stage.

b He extends the metaphor by describing men and women as actors on this stage.

c The natural time divisions in people's lives are compared to acts in a play.

2 The first age is dominated by crying and being sick.

3 a *creeping*

b His movement is compared to that of a snail.

4 The schoolboy's face could be shining because he has just had it scrubbed. (Other answers are possible here.)

5 The lover's sighs are compared to a furnace.

6 He sings praises to his lover's eyebrow.

7 A beard is compared to the hair of a leopard. This is a noble and attractive animal.

8 Shakespeare suggests that soldiers are concerned about reputation even in the face of death.

9 *bubble*